AF896454

Global Forum on Transparency and Exchange of Information for Tax Purposes Peer Reviews: Uruguay 2015

PHASE 2:
IMPLEMENTATION OF THE STANDARD IN PRACTICE

March 2015
(reflecting the legal and regulatory framework
as at December 2014)

OECD
BETTER POLICIES FOR BETTER LIVES

This work is published on the responsibility of the Secretary-General of the OECD. The opinions expressed and arguments employed herein do not necessarily reflect the official views of the OECD or of the governments of its member countries or those of the Global Forum on Transparency and Exchange of Information for Tax Purposes.

This document and any map included herein are without prejudice to the status of or sovereignty over any territory, to the delimitation of international frontiers and boundaries and to the name of any territory, city or area.

Please cite this publication as:
OECD (2015), *Global Forum on Transparency and Exchange of Information for Tax Purposes Peer Reviews: Uruguay 2015: Phase 2: Implementation of the Standard in Practice*, OECD Publishing. *http://dx.doi.org/10.1787/9789264231665-en*

ISBN 978-92-64-23165-8 (print)
ISBN 978-92-64-23166-5 (PDF)

Series: Global Forum on Transparency and Exchange of Information for Tax Purposes Peer Reviews
ISSN 2219-4681 (print)
ISSN 2219-469X (online)

Corrigenda to OECD publications may be found on line at: *www.oecd.org/publishing/corrigenda*.

© OECD 2015

You can copy, download or print OECD content for your own use, and you can include excerpts from OECD publications, databases and multimedia products in your own documents, presentations, blogs, websites and teaching materials, provided that suitable acknowledgment of OECD as source and copyright owner is given. All requests for public or commercial use and translation rights should be submitted to *rights@oecd.org*. Requests for permission to photocopy portions of this material for public or commercial use shall be addressed directly to the Copyright Clearance Center (CCC) at *info@copyright.com* or the Centre français d'exploitation du droit de copie (CFC) at *contact@cfcopies.com*.

Table of Contents

About the Global Forum

The Global Forum on Transparency and Exchange of Information for Tax Purposes is the multilateral framework within which work in the area of tax transparency and exchange of information is carried out by over 120 jurisdictions, which participate in the Global Forum on an equal footing.

The Global Forum is charged with in-depth monitoring and peer review of the implementation of the international standards of transparency and exchange of information for tax purposes. These standards are primarily reflected in the 2002 OECD Model Agreement on Exchange of Information on Tax Matters and its commentary, and in Article 26 of the OECD Model Tax Convention on Income and on Capital and its commentary as updated in 2004. The standards have also been incorporated into the UN Model Tax Convention.

The standards provide for international exchange on request of foreseeably relevant information for the administration or enforcement of the domestic tax laws of a requesting party. Fishing expeditions are not authorised but all foreseeably relevant information must be provided, including bank information and information held by fiduciaries, regardless of the existence of a domestic tax interest or the application of a dual criminality standard.

All members of the Global Forum, as well as jurisdictions identified by the Global Forum as relevant to its work, are being reviewed. This process is undertaken in two phases. Phase 1 reviews assess the quality of a jurisdiction's legal and regulatory framework for the exchange of information, while Phase 2 reviews look at the practical implementation of that framework. Some Global Forum members are undergoing combined – Phase 1 and Phase 2 – reviews. The Global Forum has also put in place a process for supplementary reports to follow-up on recommendations, as well as for the ongoing monitoring of jurisdictions following the conclusion of a review. The ultimate goal is to help jurisdictions to effectively implement the international standards of transparency and exchange of information for tax purposes.

All review reports are published once approved by the Global Forum and they thus represent agreed Global Forum reports.

For more information on the work of the Global Forum on Transparency and Exchange of Information for Tax Purposes, and for copies of the published review reports, please refer to www.oecd.org/tax/transparency and www.eoi-tax.org.

Executive Summary

1. This report summarises the legal and regulatory framework for transparency and exchange of information in Uruguay, as well as the practical implementation of that framework. The international standard which is set out in the Global Forum's Terms of Reference to Monitor and Review Progress Towards Transparency and Exchange of Information, is concerned with the availability of relevant information within a jurisdiction, the competent authority's ability to gain timely access to that information, and in turn, whether that information can be effectively exchanged with its exchange of information (EOI) partners. The assessment of effectiveness in practice has been performed in relation to a three year period (1 July 2010 through 30 June 2013).

2. After signing its first double tax convention (DTC) in 1987, Uruguay, in the five years since its 2009 commitment to implement the international standard, has been actively developing its network of information exchange mechanisms, recently signing its 31st agreement. At the same time it has begun to update its domestic laws, in particular with regards to accessing bank information, ensuring the availability of ownership information on bearer shares and to clarifying the competent authority's process for handling EOI requests.

3. The obligations requiring the retention of relevant ownership and accounting information in Uruguay are found predominantly in the Commercial Code, Business Partnerships Law (which covers companies and partnerships) and Trusts Law. These are supplemented by the regulatory system covering financial intermediaries, the anti-money laundering regime, as well as the Tax Code. In most cases, these laws create sufficient requirements to ensure the availability of ownership and identity information. However, bearer shares may still be issued by corporations and joint-stock companies. Prior to 2012, the existence of effective enforcement measures to support some of the ownership and identity obligations was not clear. Uruguay adopted Decree No. 247/012 of 2 August 2012 and Decree No. 242/012 of 1 August 2012 dealing with availability of ownership information on foreign companies and making progress in addressing the availability of ownership information for bearer shareholdings and the availability of relevant enforcement measures. In addition, Uruguay enacted Law No. 18 930

which sets out a reporting regime to address the issue of availability of ownership information in this regard.

4. To strengthen the obligations under Law 18 930, Uruguay enacted Law 19 288 published in the Official Gazette on 17 October 2014, which requires the issuing company to liquidate the interest of bearer share holders that have failed to meet their identification obligations by means of a redemption of their interest and provides a temporary mechanism of forced liquidation for non-compliant bearer share companies under certain conditions. The new Law also strengthens the identification requirements on the new bearer share holders in case of transfer. Further, whilst Law No. 18 930 provides for enforcement measures to support ownership and identity obligations in the context of a sale or assignment of ownership, in relation to bearer shareholdings and for relevant foreign companies these measures have been reinforced by Law 19 288. In practice, ownership information was available during the peer review period when requested, and obtained directly from the database of the DGI, except for one request where the information on the shareholders was obtained from the company. However, the recent laws concerning bearer shares have not been tested in practice and a Phase 2 recommendation has been included to monitor this.

5. Concerning accounting records, most entities and arrangements are subject to clear requirements to retain all relevant accounting records, including underlying documents for a 5 year minimum period. Prior to 2012, a concern arose however when an entity was not subject to tax in Uruguay, in which case the requirement to keep underlying documents for a minimum 5 year period was not clearly established. New legislation has been enacted to ensure that entities and trusts not subject to tax in Uruguay are also now legally required to maintain accounting records and underlying documents for a minimum of five years. As this legislation is recent, a monitoring recommendation has been introduced under which Uruguay should ensure that its monitoring and enforcement powers are sufficiently exercised in practice to support the legal requirements which ensure the availability of accounting information in all cases. In practice, accounting information was available during the peer review period, and obtained directly from the taxpayers.

6. The requirements to keep all relevant banking information is established by the obligations imposed on all financial intermediaries. In practice, there is active supervision of the banking system and banking information was made generally available during the peer review period in all cases where the request was considered valid.

7. Accessing information to respond to an EOI request relies upon the broad powers available to Uruguay's tax authority for domestic tax purposes. For accessing bank information, a special regime is in place which requires approval from a Court. This special regime appears to be generally effective,

but raises an issue regarding an obligation to notify the taxpayer which does not appear to be consistent with the standard. In addition, Uruguay brought into force Decree No. 313/011 which sets the procedure for exchange of information by Uruguay, under its DTCs and TIEAs. The Decree provides for prior notification to the person who is the subject of the EOI request, without any clear exception. However, a later Decree No 378/2013 dated 26 November 2013 has reduced the scope of application to Uruguayan residents, but even in such limited cases the lack of clear exceptions from this notification requirement potentially hinders effective exchange of information (e.g. in urgent cases and where such notification could harm the investigations of the requesting jurisdiction). Furthermore, under the court process for accessing bank information, certain information must be provided to the Uruguayan court to which the relevant account-holder (often the taxpayer) will have access. There are no exceptions to this notification of the account-holder prior to exchange of information. Accordingly, the two existing Phase 1 recommendations remain for the application of appropriate exceptions to ensure that the notification requirement does not hinder effective exchange of information.

8. Uruguay's exchange of information (EOI) network is based on agreements which generally follow either the OECD Model Tax Convention or the OECD Model Tax Information Exchange Agreement (Model TIEA). Uruguay has been active upgrading its EOI agreement network, with thirty-one new agreements negotiated and signed since 2009. Uruguay signed two TIEAs in 2011 and two TIEAs in 2012, which are not yet in force. Uruguay has taken all of the steps necessary to bring these into force, except for the two TIEAs signed in 2012.

9. Uruguay has made clear progress since 2009 towards implementing its commitment to the internationally agreed standard for EOI, in particular in terms of the significant progress it has made in ensuring availability of ownership information on bearer shares and in developing its network of EOI agreements with relevant partner jurisdictions. Nevertheless, there remains work to be done, in particular, there is some uncertainty about the interaction of bank secrecy provisions with effective access to information, and the interpretation by Uruguay of the entry into force provision of the EOI agreement concluded with one of its main trading partners.

10. During the period under review (July 2010 – June 2013), Uruguay received a total of 17 income tax requests for information from four jurisdictions. Out of the 17 requests, Uruguay provided the requested information in only five cases, due to a disagreement concerning the entry into force provisions for exchange of information in the TIEA concluded with an important EOI partner. The interpretation by Uruguay of the entry into force of the TIEA concluded with that EOI partner is not in line with the international standard.

11. Prior to September 2011, exchange of information operated on an ad-hoc basis in Uruguay. However, since that time, a formal EOI Unit has been implemented with set processes for all aspects related to EOI. The resources were increased by allocating staff and drafting an EOI Manual which sets out EOI procedures. The operational processes have also improved with experience.

12. Uruguay has been assigned a rating for each of the 10 essential elements as well as an overall rating. The ratings for the essential elements are based on the analysis in the text of the report, taking into account the Phase 1 determinations and any recommendations made in respect of Uruguay' legal and regulatory framework and the effectiveness of its exchange of information in practice. These ratings have been compared with the ratings assigned to other jurisdictions for each of the essential elements to ensure a consistent and comprehensive approach. On this basis, Uruguay has been assigned a rating of Compliant for elements A.3, C.2, C.3, C.4, Largely Compliant for elements A.1, A.2, C.1 and C.5, and Partially Compliant for elements B.1 and B.2. In view of the ratings for each of the essential elements taken in their entirety, the overall rating for Uruguay is Largely Compliant.

Introduction

Information and methodology used for the peer review of Uruguay

13. The original and supplementary Phase 1 assessments of the legal and regulatory framework of Uruguay were based on the international standards for transparency and exchange of information as described in the Global Forum's Terms of Reference, and were prepared using the Global Forum's Revised Methodology for Peer Reviews and Non-Member Reviews. The original Phase 1 assessment was based on the laws, regulations, and exchange of information mechanisms in force or effect as at July 2011, other materials supplied by Uruguay, and information supplied by partner jurisdictions.

14. The supplementary peer review report, which followed the original Phase 1 report of Uruguay, was prepared pursuant to paragraph 58 of the Global Forum's Methodology and was adopted by the Global Forum in October 2012. The supplementary report was based on information available to the assessment team including the laws, regulations, and exchange of information arrangements in force or effect as at August 2012, and information supplied by Uruguay.

15. The Phase 2 assessment is based on the laws, regulations, and exchange of information mechanisms in force or in effect as at 18 December 2014, Uruguay's responses to the Phase 2 questionnaire, supplementary questions and other materials supplied by Uruguay, information provided by exchange of information partners, and explanations provided by Uruguay during the on-site visit that took place from 21 to 23 July 2014 in Montevideo, Uruguay. During the on-site visit, the assessment team met with officials and representatives of the Ministry of Finance, the Large Taxpayer Division, the Taxpayer Assistance and Guidance Division, and the International Audit Department of the Uruguayan tax Administration (*Dirección General Impositiva* (DGI)), the National Register of Commerce (NRC), the Central Bank of Uruguay (*Banco Central del Uruguay* (BCU), the Notarial Council (*Asociación de Escribanos del Uruguay*), the National Internal Audit (*Auditoría Interna de la Nación* (AIN)), and the Association of Accountants (see Annex 4).

16. The following analysis reflects the Phase 1 report, as modified by the supplementary Phase 1 report approved in September 2012, and the Phase 2 assessments of the legal and regulatory framework of Uruguay in effect as at 18 December 2014, and the practical implementation and effectiveness of this framework in the three-year review period of 1 July 2010 to 30 June 2013.

17. The Terms of Reference break down the standards of transparency and exchange of information into 10 essential elements and 31 enumerated aspects under three broad categories: (A) availability of information; (B) access to information; and (C) exchanging information. This review assesses Uruguay's legal and regulatory framework and the implementation and effectiveness of this framework against these elements and each of the enumerated aspects. In respect of each essential element, a determination is made regarding Uruguay's legal and regulatory framework that either *(i)* the element is in place, *(ii)* the element is in place but certain aspects of the legal implementation of the element need improvement, or *(iii)* the element is not in place. These determinations are accompanied by recommendations on how certain aspects of the system could be strengthened, where relevant. In addition, to reflect the Phase 2 component, recommendations are made concerning Uruguay's practical application of each of the essential elements and a rating of either: *(i)* compliant, *(ii)* largely compliant, *(iii)* partially compliant, or *(iv)* non-compliant is assigned to each element. An overall rating is also assigned to reflect Uruguay's overall level of compliance with the standards. A summary of findings against those elements is set out at the end of this report.

18. The original and supplementary Phase 1 assessments were conducted by a team which consisted of two assessors and a representative of the Global Forum Secretariat: Cleve Lisecki, Attorney in the Office of Associate Chief Counsel (International) of the United States Internal Revenue Service; Alexandra Storckmeijer Sansonetti, international tax expert of the International Affairs division of the Swiss Federal Tax Authority; and Caroline Malcolm for the Phase 1 report and Ms. Doris King and Ms. Renata Fontana for the Phase 1 Supplementary Report, all members of the Global Forum Secretariat. The assessment team examined the legal and regulatory framework for transparency and exchange of information and relevant exchange of information mechanisms in Uruguay.

19. The Phase 2 assessment was conducted by an assessment team which consisted of two expert assessors and two representatives of the Global Forum Secretariat: Mr. Cleve Lisecki, Special Counsel in the Office of Division Counsel (Large Business and International) of the United States Internal Revenue Service, Mr. Daniel Ruffi, Head of Legal Assistance Service for Exchange of Information in Tax Matters (SEI), Tax Administration of Switzerland; and Ms. Séverine Baranger and Ms. Mary O'Leary from the Global Forum Secretariat. The assessment team assessed the practical

implementation and effectiveness of the legal and regulatory framework for transparency and exchange of information and relevant EOI arrangements in Uruguay.

Overview of Uruguay

General information on the economy, the legal system and the taxation system

20. The Republic of Uruguay (Uruguay; *República Oriental del Uruguay*) is located in South America, bordered by the Republic of Argentina, Brazil and the Atlantic Ocean. It has a population of just fewer than 3.4 million people, with 85% living in urban areas including the approximately 1.3 million people living in the capital, Montevideo. The national currency is the Uruguayan peso, which at 30 June 2014 was valued at USD 0.0437. Uruguay is one of the most economically developed countries in South America, with a relatively high and steadily increasing GDP per capita. In 2013, the total GDP equalled USD 55 708 million, which was approximately USD 16 500 per capita.

21. The Uruguayan Constitution (1967) establishes a democratic republic with a presidential system. State power is divided between the legislature, executive and judiciary. Parliament is divided into the Chamber of Senators and the Chamber of Deputies. Representatives of both Chambers and the President of Uruguay are each elected by direct universal suffrage for 5 year terms.

22. The executive branch of government is led by the President, and 13 cabinet ministers (who make up the Council of Ministers). For governance purposes, Uruguay is divided into 19 administrative departments which each have a government led by the "Intendente" (elected by direct popular vote), and a council (formed by the mayors of each of the cities in the department). The third tier of government is the municipalities, which are organised with a Mayor and council.

23. The judiciary is headed by the Supreme Court of Justice, with 5 judges appointed by the government for 10 year terms. Legal challenges to a decision of an officer of the Tax Administration Authority (*Dirección General Impositiva* (DGI)) are made first to the DGI who issued the decision (an appeal for reconsideration) and in the same document as a subsidiary petition, to their superior within the Public Administration (a hierarchy appeal). If the original decision is upheld by those appeals, the person may appeal to the Administrative Appeals Tribunal (Tribunal de lo Contencioso Administrativo) to determine whether the decision from the

Public Administration is incorrect or unlawful. This Court can only confirm or reject (but not modify) the original decision. When the claim is made on constitutional grounds, the appeal is to be made to the Supreme Court.[1]

24. Uruguay has a civil law legal system, with a hierarchy of laws as follows: the Constitution; laws (including "decree-laws"[2]); and decrees, regulations and resolutions. Laws must be passed by the parliament, whilst decrees, regulations and resolutions are prepared and enacted by the Council of Ministers, and promulgated by the President. In addition, the regional governments can issue decrees, and municipalities may issue resolutions. The jurisdiction of those decrees and resolutions is confined to the corresponding department or municipality and they cannot override a law, decree, regulation or resolution of the national government. International treaties, including double tax conventions (DTCs) and tax information exchange agreements (TIEAs) have the same status as laws made by the national government. Uruguay has advised that there is an implied principle derived from articles 9 and 10 of the Civil Code that where there is a conflict between laws, the most recent will prevail.

25. Under Article 10 of the Civil Code, new laws prevail over provisions of older laws that cannot be reconciled with the new laws. The repeal of the previous law may be explicitly mentioned in the new law, or may be simply implicit from the provisions which cannot be reconciled with the previous law. The Uruguayan authorities have confirmed that this principle has not created uncertainty in the application of the law.

26. The key economic sectors in Uruguay, understood in terms of their contribution to gross domestic product (GDP, being USD 55708 million in 2013), include services (other than financial services, 39.6%), commerce (including restaurants and hotels, 13.1%), manufacturing (11%), construction (8.9%) and agriculture (8.2 %). Financial intermediation contributed only 2% to the total GDP in 2010. Uruguay's main export partners are Brazil 19.1%, China 16%, Nueva Palmira Free Zone (one of Uruguay's free trade zones – see further paragraph 32 below), Venezuela 4 4.9%,, Germany 4% and US 3.9%; whilst it predominantly sources imports from China 20.2%, Brazil 17.4%, Argentina 17%, US 9% and Mexico 3.1%.

1. Section XVII Uruguayan Constitution.
2. Under Uruguayan law, "decree-law" refers to the regulation issued during the last civil and military dictatorship which ruled from 1973-85, and which were the only form of regulation available, since there was no parliament in operation. Upon the return of the democratically elected government, some of these laws were validated by the parliament (Law 15 738), and they are now known as decrees with the force of law. Those decree-laws which have not been so validated, are no longer legally binding.

27. The national tax system in Uruguay is administered by the DGI. The principal national taxes are:

- Company tax (IRAE) – imposed on companies and individuals, either resident or with permanent establishment, on Uruguayan source income (including capital gains) originating from industrial, commercial and agricultural activities.[3] Standard rate is 25%.
- Non-Resident Income Tax (IRNR) – imposed on Uruguayan source income obtained by non-resident individuals.
- Personal tax (IRPF) – imposed on Uruguayan source income including income from capital gains. The rate is imposed based on whether it is category I (income from capital and capital gains) or category II (income from dependent or independent personal services and pensions). Tax rates on different types of category I income vary, but are flat; whilst the rate for category II income is progressive.
- Wealth tax (IP) – payable by corporations and individuals, with an exemption for agricultural activities, up to USD 1 500 000. Where the entity also pays the company tax, net worth tax is imposed at the standard rate of 1.5% of net worth.
- VAT – is imposed on goods and services at the basic rate of 22%. Certain exemptions exist, either in entirety, or to apply a reduced rate of 10%.

28. At the provincial level, the main taxes are a real property tax, vehicle registration fee and a food analysis tax.

29. A person is considered to be a Uruguayan resident for tax purposes if they are present in Uruguay for more than 183 days in a calendar year; or if directly or indirectly the economic activities or individual interests (e.g. family) of the person are located in Uruguay. Companies are considered resident when they are incorporated under Uruguayan law. Foreign companies that have a permanent establishment in Uruguay (which is defined in article 10 of the Company Tax Law) are only taxable on their Uruguayan-source income. Partnerships and trusts are taxed on an entity basis (except for guarantee trusts) under Uruguayan law.

30. In general, foreign-source income is not taxable under Uruguayan law. However, in 2011 new legislation was introduced which will tax individuals on income realised from foreign passive investments.

3. In the case of income derived from agricultural activities, certain entities may elect to be subject to either the usual company tax, or to the tax on disposal of agricultural goods.

31. Uruguay also operates twelve free trade zones (FTZs), which are areas within the national territory which confer certain tax exemptions and other benefits for commercial activities carried out therein. A specific type of company (SAZF, Sociedad Anónima de Zona Franca) may be incorporated (article 17, Law 15 921) which are permitted to operate only in these zones, and overseas. Users of the FTZs benefit not only from an exemption from customs duty, but also from an exemption from national taxation including income tax, present or future, with regard to the activities carried out in the FTZ. SAZFs are required to be registered in the National Registry of Commerce (NRC).

Overview of commercial laws and other relevant factors for exchange of information

32. Under Uruguayan law, the list of entities recognised as separate legal entities include trading companies (corporations, limited liability companies, joint stock companies, limited partnerships), economic interest groups (similar to a corporate group, with separate legal personality), co-operative corporations, mutual guarantee corporations and foundations. Some other legal structures, such as trusts, do not have legal personality.

33. Entities with separate legal personality may be formed in two main ways: upon execution of an agreement (e.g. for trading companies, economic interest groups); or, upon the authorisation of, or registration with, a relevant government authority (e.g. for co-operative corporations and associations).

Overview of the financial sector and relevant professions

34. The financial sector in Uruguay consisted of "financial" and "non-financial" institutions. As of January 2014, the financial institutions included 14 commercial banks (2 state-owned and 12 private, foreign-owned banks), 1 co-operative financial institution, 5 finance houses ("casas financieras"), 3 offshore financial institutions ("instituciones financieras externas" or "IFEs"), and 4 pension funds managing companies. In addition, non-financial institutions are the institutions managing credit (14), exchange houses (58) and companies providing financial services (26). The last group, companies providing financial services, may carry out funds transfers, payments and collections, and rent safe deposit boxes, as well as provide currency exchange services and other activities.

35. Each type of institution is restricted to carrying out certain activities according to its type. The three key types of "financial institutions" are the commercial banks, the financial houses and the IFEs, and the scope of their activities is described here. Commercial banks may:

- Receive current account deposits and authorise drawings thereupon by means of cheques;
- Receive at-call deposits from residents and receive at-call deposits in local currency from non-residents; and
- Receive term deposits from residents.

36. Financial houses are defined as those companies authorised to carry out any kind of financial intermediation activities, except those reserved to commercial banks. Hence, financial houses are allowed to:

- accept term deposits (over 30 days) from non-residents, either in foreign or local currency; and
- accept at-call deposits (less than 30 days) from non-residents, in foreign currency.

37. Finally, IFEs are created under Article 4 of Decree Law 15 322 and are defined as those entities whose only corporate purpose consists in carrying out intermediation activities with non-residents only, or within Uruguayan free trade zones, regarding the offer and demand of securities, money or precious metals located abroad (or in the free-trade zones).

38. At the beginning of 2014, commercial banks held 97.9% of total assets in the financial system, with 43.7% held by the two state-owned banks. Other financial institutions such as the IFEs and finance houses held the remainder. In March 2014, total deposits held in the financial and non-financial institutions reached USD 32 463 million, of which non-resident deposits amounted to USD 3 892 million accounting for 12.2 %. Although in 2002 a banking crisis in Uruguay saw the loss of 40% of banking deposits and the closure of a number of banks, since then the financial sector has recovered steadily.

39. All professional trustees, investment funds and pension funds are regulated by the Central Bank of Uruguay (*Banco Central del Uruguay* (BCU)). Investment funds are formed by contributions of individuals or legal persons, administered by a corporation with registered shares who has similar obligations to those of a trustee. As at 1 October 2014, there were 16 investment funds regulated by the BCU. Pension funds (Retirement Funds Savings Managing Companies, AFAPs) are a specific type of investment fund, which have as their objective the placement of social security savings of their shareholders. As at 1 October 2014, there were 4 pension funds regulated by the BCU.

40. Anti-money laundering measures were introduced in 2000, with the introduction of regulations by the BCU which *inter alia* created the Financial Research and Analysis Unit (IUAF) within the BCU to report on suspicious

transactions. In 2004, parliament sanctioned the regulatory measures introduced by the bank in 2000, passing Law 17 835 which included obligations on the financial sector as well as designated professions and persons carrying out certain activities, to report suspicious activities. In 2007, the National Anti-Money Laundering Agency and the Coordination Committee against money laundering were created.

Recent developments

41. On 26 September 2014, the Uruguayan Parliament adopted Law 19 288 which strengthens the provisions of Law 18 930 on the reporting system on the ownership of bearer shares. Law 19 288 entered into force on 1 November 2014. Law 19 288 aims to address some gaps identified in the Phase 1 supplementary report through two mechanisms:

(i) the dissolution by operation of the law of the issuing entities failing to meet the requirements to report about the owners of bearer shares who represent at least 50% of the paid-up capital within 90 days after the entry into force of Law 19.288 (i.e. 29 January 2015); and

(ii) at any time, a loss of status as shareholder in case the bearer shareholder has not met its ownership information requirements.

The aim of Law 19 288 is to ensure that after the 90-day period following the adoption of Law 19 288, there should not be any unidentified bearer shares in Uruguay.

42. Uruguay signed TIEAs with Guernsey on 2 July 2014 and Chile on 12 September 2014 and a DTC with the United Arab Emirates in October 2014, bringing its total number of signed agreements to 31. Uruguay ratified the TIEA concluded with Brazil on 22 December 2014, by way of Law 19 303.

Compliance with the Standards

A. Availability of Information

Overview

43. Effective exchange of information requires the availability of reliable information. In particular, it requires information on the identity of owners and other stakeholders as well as information on the transactions carried out by entities and other organisational structures. Such information may be kept for tax, regulatory, commercial or other reasons. If the information is not kept or it is not maintained for a reasonable period of time, a jurisdiction's competent authority may not be able to obtain and provide it when requested. This section of the report assesses the adequacy of Uruguay's legal and regulatory framework on the availability of information.

44. Uruguayan law permits the creation of a number of different types of companies and partnerships (which fall within a broader grouping known as "business partnerships") under the Business Partnerships Law. There are effective requirements in place to ensure the availability of ownership and identity information in respect of these entities. Bearer shares may be issued by most corporations (including free-trade zone corporations) and joint-stock companies.

45. Uruguay has enacted Law No. 18 930 of 17 July 2012 and adopted two accompanying decrees, which are collectively designed to ensure the availability of ownership information on foreign companies and bearer shares. Law No. 18 930 sets out an ownership reporting regime in relation to bearer shares and for foreign companies which are either effectively managed or conduct

business through a permanent establishment in Uruguay. The ownership reporting obligations introduced by Law No. 18 930 and Decree No. 247/012 on foreign companies having sufficient nexus with Uruguay conforms to the standard.

46. In addition, Law No. 18 930 provides for: *(i)* the registration of the sale or assignment of ownership in business partnerships (which includes both companies and partnerships), associations and agricultural partnerships with the Uruguayan tax authorities; *(ii)* reporting obligations in relation to nominee holdings of bearer equity; and *(iii)* requirement for the maintenance of accounting records and underlying documentation in relation to trusts which are not supervised by the Uruguayan Central Bank (BCU). Decree No. 242/012 of 1 August 2012 amends Decree No. 597/988 to provide specific timeframes for the registration of transfer of ownership in, amongst others, business partnerships (which includes both companies and partnerships) other than corporations with the DGI. Decree No. 242/012 also sets out a requirement for entities not subject to Uruguayan tax to maintain underlying accounting documentation for five years. Recently, Law 19 288 has strengthened the reporting requirements and enforcement measures on bearer shares set-out by Law No 18 930, thereby addressing the concerns identified in the Supplementary Phase 1 report concerning Law No 18 930.

47. The bearer share reporting regime set out by Law No. 18 930, Law 19 288 and Decrees No. 247/012 and No. 346/014 provides for reporting obligations in relation to existing bearer shareholdings, and also upon transfer and new issuance of bearer shares. Stringent penalties apply to both non-compliant shareholders and issuing entities. In addition, Law 19 288 has answered the concerns arising in some cases that transfers of bearer shareholdings, could remain undetected and ownership information could remain unavailable to the Uruguay tax authorities. Under Law 19 288, resident entities failing to meet the requirements to report the owners of bearer shares who represent at least 50% of the paid-up capital within 90 days within the entry into force of Law 19 288 (i.e. 29 January 2015) will be dissolved. Bearer shareholders not meeting their separate reporting obligations will lose their shareholder status. Their interest will be liquidated and the proceeds of liquidation will be distributed to them. The fines for non-compliance with the reporting requirements must be collected from the distribution by the distributing company and paid to AIN. Failure to comply with this requirement will make the distributing company severally liable for the amount of the fine.

48. For trusts, there are clear requirements to keep identity information in respect of settlors, trustees and beneficiaries, and no issues have been found in practice. Whilst foundations may be created under Uruguayan law, they are limited to non-profit activities, and thus their significance is limited. In addition, there are a number of entities and arrangements which may be

formed such as economic interest groups, informal partnerships and consortiums; in each of these cases they are subject to requirements to maintain relevant ownership and identity information in line with the standard. In practice, Uruguay did not receive requests regarding ownership information on trusts, foundations or any of these other economic arrangements during the peer review period.

49. The measures to ensure the effective enforcement of these obligations to maintain ownership and identity information are generally in place. Law No. 18 930 together with Decree No. 242/012 and Decree No. 247/012 provide for enforcement provisions to support a new obligation to register transfers of ownership in companies (excluding corporations) and partnerships with the Uruguayan tax authorities prior to the registration of such information with the NRC, and also to support provisions to ensure the availability of ownership information for foreign companies and in relation to bearer shareholdings. In practice, monitoring activities and enforcement measures have been found adequate to ensure availability of information in case of transfers of ownership in companies (excluding corporations) and partnerships due to the mandatory involvement of a public notary to register the transfer of ownership. In addition, adequate monitoring procedures and activities have been carried out for the effective implementation of Law 18 930, with a specific commission being established for the implementation of Law 18 930 and a close co-operation taking place with other relevant governmental agencies; such as the BCU and the DGI.

50. Uruguay identified a gap in practice following the implementation of Law 18 930, with approximately 75 000 inactive bearer share companies which had not complied with the provisions of Law 18 930[4]. However, Uruguay addressed this serious gap by enacting Law 19 288, which would dissolve all non-compliant eligible inactive bearer share companies on 29 January 2015. Although Uruguay has carried out a sound implementation and monitoring program of Law 18 930, Uruguay should continue to monitor the availability of ownership information on bearer shares under Law 18 930 and Law 19 288.

51. In practice, Uruguay received two requests for ownership information during the peer review period concerning direct taxes. Uruguay provided the requested information; one regarding the identity of shareholders of a bearer share company and another request regarding non bearer share companies. Uruguay received an additional 11 VAT requests which included

4. The Uruguayan authorities have clarified that they arrived at this number by taking the number of bearer share companies that used to be registered with the DGI at some point but lost their status of active companies, and did not enter into liquidation (see section A.1.2 *Bearer Shares*).

requests for ownership information, which are not evaluated for the purpose of this report.

52. Overall, considering the enactment of Law 18 930 on ownership and identity information concerning bearer shares and enforcement measures and Law 19 288 published in the Official Gazette on 17 October 2014, the Phase 1 determination of element A.1 is found to be "in place". In light of the considerable resources allocated to addressing the concerns regarding the availability of information on bearer shares, the implementation program of Law 19 288 and the availability of ownership information on bearer shares in one case when asked, the overall rating for Element A.1 is determined to be "Largely Compliant".

53. In respect of accounting records, broad obligations which cover most relevant entities and arrangements stem from the Tax Code, and ensure in most instances that reliable accounting records, including underlying documentation are required to be kept for a minimum of five years. These obligations are supplemented by additional obligations in the Commercial Code, the Business Partnerships Law and through the regulation of financial intermediaries. Decree No. 242/012 introduces for entities, which are not subject to tax in Uruguay, an obligation to maintain underlying records for a minimum period of 5 years. It also sets out an obligation for trusts not subject to tax in Uruguay to maintain accounting records and underlying documentation for a minimum period of 5 years. The record retention requirement set out in Decree No. 242/012 is supplemented by obligations under the Uruguayan Central Bank (BCU) regulations and section 23 of Law No. 18 930, which provide respectively for trusts (whether subject to tax or otherwise) to maintain underlying documentation for ten years. Element A.2 is found to be "in place". In practice, Uruguay received 19 requests for accounting information during the peer review period but 12 of them concerned VAT and therefore fall out of the scope of this review. Accounting information was provided in three cases regarding companies out of the seven income tax cases. The non-provision of accounting information in four cases pertained to matters regarding the entry into force provision of one EOI agreement (see section C.1 *Exchange-of-information mechanisms*), and not to availability of accounting information. However, experience of monitoring the accounting obligations set out in Decree No. 242/012 dated 1 August 2012 and filing obligations contained in article 24 of Law 18 930, which apply since August 2012 to entities not subject to tax, is limited. In the circumstances, Uruguay should ensure that its monitoring and enforcement powers are sufficiently exercised in practice to ensure the availability of accounting information in these cases. Therefore, Uruguay is rated "Largely Compliant" on element A.2.

54. Banks, as well as other persons carrying out financial intermediation activities, are subject to regulation by the BCU. This regulation establishes comprehensive client identity information requirements, as well as transaction record requirements. result The Phase 1 determination of element A.3 is found to be in place. The BCU has a good monitoring program in place, and has carried out onsite inspections during the peer review period. Uruguay has received ten requests regarding banking information. Although banking information is generally available in Uruguay it was not provided in five cases. The non-provision of banking information in these cases pertained to matters regarding access to banking information (see section B.1 *Competent Authority's ability to obtain and provide information*) or to the interpretation of the entry into force provision of one EOI agreement (see section C.1 *Exchange-of-information mechanisms*), and not to availability of banking information. Accordingly, element A.3 is rated "Compliant".

A.1. Ownership and identity information

Jurisdictions should ensure that ownership and identity information for all relevant entities and arrangements is available to their competent authorities.

Companies (ToR A.1.1)

Types of Companies

55. Companies are types of "business partnerships" under Uruguayan Law, and may take one of the forms described in article 3 of the Law 16 060 (the Business Partnerships Law). These include:

1. Limited Liability Companies (*Sociedad de Responsabilidad Limitada* (SRL), Ch II, Sect. IV): capital divided into shares, which may not be represented by negotiable instruments. Liability of members is limited to their contribution, and the number of members shall not exceed 50 (upon exceeding this number, it shall change into a Corporation within 2 years). They may not issue bearer shares. As of 30 June 2014, there were 25 808 active SRL, registered with the DGI in Uruguay.
2. Corporations (*Sociedad Anónima* (SA), Ch II, Sect. V): capital is divided into shares, which may be represented by negotiable instruments and be in nominative, bearer[5] or book-entry form (article 304; on bearer shares). Liability of shareholders is limited to the share

5. Neither bearer shares nor bearer coupons maybe issued by "open" (for public subscription) corporations.

value. Corporations may be open[6] and therefore regulated by the state control body, or closed (being all other corporations which are not "open": article 248, Business Partnerships Law). Coupons may be issued which relate to earnings or other rights, and these may be bearer coupons even in the case of nominative shares (article 302). Free Trade Zone Corporations (SAZFs, governed largely pursuant to Law 15 921) are a sub-type of corporation and subject to the same relevant requirements in respect of ownership and identity information. As of 30 June 2014, there were 19 657 active SAs with nominative shares, 37 596 SAs with bearer shares and 33 with book-entry shares registered with the DGI.[7]

3. Joint Stock Companies (*Sociedad en Comandita por Acciones* (SCA), Ch II, Sect. VI): capital is divided into shares, which may be represented by negotiable instruments (article 474, Business Partnerships Law). Active partners (*socios comanditados o gestores*) have unlimited liability, whilst special partners (*socios comanditarios*) are only liable to the extent of their contributions. The obligations relevant to limited partnership apply, except in respect of special partners and their share capital, where the provisions regarding corporations apply (including that they may issue bearer shares). As of 30 June 2014, there were 123 active SCA with bearer shares and 51 SCA with nominative shares, registered with the DGI.

Information available with the Uruguayan authorities

56. Article 6 of the Business Partnerships Law provides that a deed constituting a business partnership will be made, and it must contain information including:

- the name and address of the business partnership; and
- accurate identification of those entering into the contract [i.e. the founding members] and their capital contributions.

6. A corporation which resorts to public savings to constitute their original capital or to increase it and who quote their shares in the stock market or obtain loans through the public issuance of negotiable obligations (article 247, Business Partnerships Law).
7. Reference is made to Section A.1.6 *Enforcement Provisions to Ensure Availability of Information* with respect to the number of passive bearer share SAs, and those bearer shares SAs, the capital of which was converted into nominative shares after 30 June 2013.

Registration with the National Register of Commerce

57. All companies (including foreign companies, as well as co-operatives, economic interest groups and consortiums) are required to register the deed constituting their business partnership (for example, contract of incorporation) in the National Register of Commerce (NRC) pursuant to article 49(2) of the NRC Law 16 871 (NRC Law). All modifications to the initial incorporation deed, which Uruguay has advised includes any subsequent transfers of shares in a company except corporations, are also required to be registered in the NRC (article 49(6), NRC Law). These transfers are notified and published in the company file. The NRC is controlled by the General Registries Office within the Ministry of Education and Culture. These provisions regarding identification of shareholders will not apply in respect of any bearer shares which may be issued, as these are subject to specific reporting requirements (see further below section A.1.2 for the report on Bearer shares).

Registration in practice

58. All business entities (including all domestic or foreign companies), being companies or not, have to follow the same registration procedure. To incorporate a business entity in Uruguay, the first step is the registration of the deed of incorporation with a public notary, who keeps the information in a notary register. The notary registers are inspected on an annual basis by a dedicated government agency (*Inspección General de Registros Notariales*) and are subject to stringent AML obligations[8].

59. Subsequently, the business entity must be registered with the NRC, which is given the incorporation deed, certified by the public notary. All registrations are carried out in person, usually by the public notary at a local office of the NRC. The registration at the NRC can also be carried out by other persons, such as a company director, but this possibility is less used in practice.

60. The NRC first checks the validity of the incorporation deed as certified by the public notary to ensure that it complies with all of the legal requirements. The NRC also checks that the business entity has previously been issued with a Tax Identification Number (*Registro Unico Tributario*, RUT[9]) and carries out a name search. Applying for and obtaining a taxpayer identification number is a prerequisite for business entities' registration in Uruguay (see section on Registration with the Tax Administration Authority).

---

8. Notaries are subject to customer due diligence requirements under Uruguayan anti-money laundering legislation and must identify the beneficial owner in any document they authorise (Article 9, AML/FT Decree No 355/010).
9. Article 80 of Law 16 462.

The NRC then issues a certificate indicating that the business entity is registered for business purposes. All filed information is publicly available against a fee, and includes amongst others, the identity of the founders, and the updated ownership information of members of limited liability companies (SRLs) and partnerships (i.e. personal companies). The registration fee amounts to approximately USD 100.

61. The NRC registers any change or amendments in the bylaws, except for transfers of corporation's shares. With respect to the members of personal companies, the transfer of member's interests does not have any legal effects if they are not registered with the NRC. Under Article 22 of Law 18 930, the sale of interests in personal companies must be registered with the DGI before registration to the NRC. The notaries public usually carry out the arrangements of informing the DGI and the NRC of changes and amendments in the bylaws.

62. There are approximately 40 staff members within the NRC. Staff members verify that all legal requirements (such as the registration with the DGI) have been fulfilled before validating a registration or a change in the bylaws. All documents registered with the NRC are kept indefinitely.

Registration with the Tax Administration Authority

63. All entities, including companies incorporated under Uruguayan law, as well as foreign companies subject to tax in Uruguay (those carrying on business through a permanent establishment in Uruguay) are required to register with the DGI at the time of starting or restarting taxable activity providing to the DGI the "information and documents that are required" (article 9, Decree 597/988). Uruguay has advised that this required information will include the provision of certain information (such as the bylaws of the companies), which must be kept up to date, including the company's full name and business address, although not complete ownership information.

64. Registration for tax purposes consist of the completion of a RUT (*Registro Unico Tributario*) form, to get a tax identification number. The form is then processed by the DGI which generates a RUT number for proposed officers of the company or the yet to be registered business entity. These RUT formalities must be carried out before the registration of the business entity with the NRC, and are therefore an effective means by which to ensure all entities are registered for both tax and business purposes.

65. Section 22 of Law No. 18 930 of July 2012 sets out a new requirement for the registration of sale of stakeholdings in SRL and partnerships with the DGI prior to registration of such transfer with the General Registries Office which controls the NRC. This is supplemented by Decree No. 247/012 which provides that registration of such sale and assignment with the DGI must

occur within 30 days of the contract of sale or assignment (s. 1 of Decree No. 242/012, inserting s. 30(bis) in Decree No. 597/988). Section 22 does not cover SAs or SCAs.

66. In practice, a taxpayer needs to first register the transfer of interest of a SRL or partnership with the DGI, before registering the transfer with the notary and the NRC. In addition, the transfer must be registered with the public notary, before being recorded with the NRC. The NRC does not allow the registration of the transfer of stakeholdings in limited liability companies and partnerships without the certificate from the public notary. This new registration requirement is supported by enforcement provisions under the Tax Code (see A.1.6 below). According to the above, the ownership identity of SRLs or partnership is available with the notary, the DGI and the NRC. Transfers of nominal shares of a corporation (SA or SCA) are not subject to registration with the DGI or the NRC, but they must be recorded in the register of shareholders required to be kept by these companies (see below).

Information available with the companies

67. The Business Partnerships Law also establishes obligations on the companies themselves to maintain records of share ownership as follows:

- Limited Liability Companies (SRLs (articles 231 and 232, Business Partnerships Law)): assignments of shares to existing owners may be freely undertaken (except where it affects the majority holdings). Assignment to third parties may not be undertaken unless shareholders holding 75% of the share capital agree (prior-notification of the intent to transfer must be given, and no response within 15 days indicates consent). There is no express requirement for the company itself to notify this transfer to existing members, or keep a record.
- (SAs): closed corporations are subject to an obligation to keep a share register for nominative shares, as well as a register for any book-entry shares that are issued (articles 333 and 334, Business Partnerships Law). Transfers of nominative or book-entry shares are not valid until they are registered in the register that is required to be kept by closed corporations (article 305, Business Partnerships Law). The obligations of corporation regarding bearer shares are set out in section A.1.2. Corporations which are carrying out financial intermediation activities[10] are required to include in their statute a provision that only nominative shares shall be issued (article 43, Law 15 322).
- Joint Stock Companies (SCAs): the transfer of a share holding of an active partner (article 482, Business Partnerships Law) must be

10. See section A.1.3.

approved by an absolute majority and must be recorded in the share register of the SCA. The transfer of a share holding of a special partner follows the rules applicable to corporations.

68. The availability of ownership information relies on the registration obligations with the public notary for incorporations and for the transfer of interest in all companies, except SAs and SCAs. Without this notary intervention, the company cannot register the incorporation or the changes in ownership with the NRC and with the DGI. Notaries public are subject to stringent AML requirements. For SAs and SCAs, the ownership information is required to be kept by the company (with an update of the shareholder register) and is therefore available. In sum therefore, all types of companies formed under the Business Partnerships Law are subject to requirements under that law, AML laws and the NRC Law which ensure records are kept identifying nominative owners.

Foreign companies

69. Foreign companies which carry on a business in Uruguay through a permanent establishment are required to register in the NRC including providing their contract of incorporation, and meet the obligations relating to ownership information described above (article 193, Business Partnerships Law). Before 2012, these foreign companies were not expressly required to provide identity information concerning their owners as a part of registration requirements with the NRC. Instead, the availability of ownership information depended on the law of the jurisdiction in which the company was formed and it could not be available in all cases.

70. However, Law No. 18 930 of 17 July 2012 and Decree No. 247/012 of 2 August 2012 established an ownership reporting mechanism for bearer shares and any form of shares issued by foreign entities which either have their place of effective management in Uruguay or conduct business through a permanent establishment in Uruguay (ss. 2 and 6 of Law No. 18 930; s. 1(II) of Decree No. 247/012). Pursuant to this reporting regime (see below Section A.1.2 on Bearer shares for details), these relevant foreign entities are required to provide information to the BCU on the identity of their owners within 120 days of the effective date of Law No. 18 930, i.e. by 1 December 2012 (s. 19 of Decree No. 247/012). Furthermore, such relevant foreign entities must report all changes in ownership to the BCU within 30 days of receipt of such information (s. 8 of Decree No. 247/012).

71. These reporting requirements are supported by a range of sanctions which apply to non-compliant foreign companies: administrative fines apply to both the non-compliant entities and to their representatives (to the extent of their culpability), which are set out in A.1.6.

Ownership information on foreign companies in practice

72. The Uruguayan authorities have stated that foreign companies are involved in the financial sectors, tannery and laboratories. Uruguay has received one request regarding ownership information on a foreign company, to which it responded successfully, but the request dealt with VAT matters.

73. The registration of the foreign company with the NRC will require a public notary, who will be in charge of gathering all the necessary information for registration with the NRC (see about section on *Registration in practice*).

74. With respect to the ownership identification requirements of foreign companies in Uruguay, the BCU has two types of forms; one has to be filed by the foreign company and the other one by its shareholders. These forms can be submitted by the directors of the foreign companies in Uruguay. However, in practice, the public notary, which takes care of the affairs of the foreign company in Uruguay (for example, the one who took care of the registration with the NRC), sends the information digitally with a token dedicated to foreign companies information. The public notary is responsible for getting the signature of the representative of the foreign companies and the attestation of the public notary.

75. With respect to monitoring the registration obligations, the BCU and the AIN concluded a Memorandum of Understanding to govern the exchange of information between the two authorities. This allows the BCU to notify the AIN of any non-compliance. The AIN, in turn, applies the penalties for failure to comply with the registration requirements. Some information is sent automatically by the BCU, whereas other types of information are provided upon request. As of 9 June 2014, 125 foreign companies were registered with the BCU. The BCU crossed-checked its database with the database of the DGI. The DGI has 650 foreign companies in its database, such that the remaining 525 foreign companies were infringing Law 18 930. Compliance action is now being taken (see section A.1.6 for more details).

76. For EOI requests on ownership information of foreign companies, the DGI has direct access into the BCU register according to article 5 of Law 18 930.

Nominees

77. The concept of nominee shareholding and the distinction between legal and beneficial ownership that exist in some jurisdictions, in particular common law jurisdictions, does not exist in Uruguayan law. The legal owner of registered shares of companies registered in Uruguay is in principle considered to be the beneficial owner.

78. The concepts of *mandatario* and *carta poder* do exist in Uruguayan law, however, these are quite different from the concept of nominee ownership. *Mandatarios* are persons acting as long term representatives of a shareholder, whose scope of representation is specified in the power of attorney under which such power is granted. Holders of *carta poder* are persons acting as short term representatives of a shareholder (such as for one specific meeting which the shareholder is unable to attend); his/her scope of representation is set out in a letter executed by a notary, in relation to a specific occasion. Specifically, neither a *mandatario* nor a holder of *carta poder* is the legal or beneficial owner of shares.

79. In any event, identity information relating to the principal of a *mandatario* or *carta poder* arrangement (i.e. the shareholder) will be documented and available. Both types of documentation through which powers of representation are granted must be prepared by a notary, who is subject to customer due diligence requirements under Uruguayan anti-money laundering legislation to identify the beneficial owner in any document they authorise (Article 9, AML/FT Decree No 355/010). Accordingly, both the power of attorney (in relation to *mandatarios*) and the letter in relation to grant of power to a holder of *carta poder* must state identity information in relation to both the principal and the representative, including their names, addresses, identity numbers and nationalities (Public Notaries Regulations, Title IV, Chapter I, s. 130). Such documents must be filed with the company prior to attendance by the representative at the relevant shareholders' meeting (Business Partnerships Law, ss. 350 and 351). In this regard, the evolved view of the Global Forum on this issue of *mandatarios*, as reflected in other reports adopted since Uruguay's Phase 1 supplementary review, is noted.

80. Law No. 18 930 provides that representatives acting on behalf of owners of bearer shares issued by Uruguayan entities and any form of shares issued by relevant foreign entities must report to the issuing entity identification information in relation to "the security owner and anyone who develop the functions of holding, custody or representation" (ss. 1 and 2). Uruguayan authorities indicated that the representatives contemplated as within the scope of this obligation are *mandatarios* and holders of *carta poder*, consistent with the understanding of these concepts under Uruguayan law as described above.

81. In practice, it is common in Uruguay to use a "*Carta Poder*" or a "*Mandato*". The *Carta poder* is a private document signed by the principal. It is used in general for one particular transaction (for example to carry out some formalities with the customs office). The "*Mandato*" is a public document, which is registered with the public register of notary and is of more permanent nature (for example to buy an immovable property). In each case, the public notary must clearly establish the identity of the *mandatorio* and

"*apoderado*", and shall request the general power of attorney given to the *mandatario* and *apoderado* by the principal. The notaries are bound by law to report suspicious transactions to the BCU. The supervision of these obligations is with the Ministry of Finance together with the BCU.

82. During the peer review period, Uruguay did not receive any requests pertaining to a *carta poder* or a *mandato*.

Bearer shares (ToR A.1.2)

83. Closed corporations (SAs) (i.e. corporations which are not open for public subscription) and joint stock corporations (SCAs), as well as free trade zone companies, may issue bearer shares, as well as bearer coupons (the latter in respect of nominative, book-entry and bearer shares). Since 31 August 2007 bearer shares are prohibited from being issued by some types of companies, being SAs or SCAs which hold property rights over rural estates or carry out agricultural activities (Law 18 172). These entities were given a 2-year period from August 2007 in which to convert the bearer shares into parts or nominative shares, whose owners must be individuals. Failure to do resulted in the termination of the SA or SCA by operation of law (article 349, Law 18 172).

84. Bearer shares may be issued by closed SAs, SCAs and free trade zone companies, and until 2012, there was no mechanism in place to ensure that the owners of bearer shares or coupons could be identified in all instances. Law No. 18 930 of 17 July 2012 and Decree No. 247/012 of 2 August 2012 ("the 2012 laws) established an ownership reporting mechanism for bearer shares issued by Uruguayan resident entities (as well as other bearer instruments including bonds, beneficial participation notes and coupons) and any form of shares issued by foreign entities which have their place of effective management, or conduct business through a permanent establishment, in Uruguay (ss. 1 and 2 of Law No. 18 930). In both cases, where representatives act on behalf of the share owners, they are required to provide identity information in relation to the persons on whose behalf they act. The term "entities" includes trusts and investment funds. The reporting obligations apply in relation to both relevant shares existing at the effective date of Law No. 18 930 (i.e. 1 August 2012), as well as new issuances after this date. The 2012 Laws also set out a specific regime for corporations converting their share capital in bearer shares into nominative shares. Publicly listed companies and companies that entirely transform their issued bearer shares into registered shares by 1 October 2012, i.e. within 60 days of the effective date of Law No. 18 930, are exempt from the reporting obligations (ss. 15 and 17 of Law No. 18 930; s. 20 of Decree No. 247/012).

85. In addition, Uruguay adopted Law 19 288 published on 17 October 2014 in the Official Gazette, which strengthens the reporting mechanisms set out in the 2012 laws, and addresses uncertainties that remained following their adoption, as highlighted in Phase 1 supplementary report. One of the main goals of Law 19 288 is to ensure the liquidation by operation of law of inactive bearer share companies, for which the provisions of Law 18 930 proved insufficient (see section on *Mechanisms introduced by New Law 19 288*).

Reporting mechanism under the 2012 Laws

86. The following reporting mechanisms were established for bearer shares by the Law No. 18 930:

- Shareholders must report to the issuing entity, within 60 days of Law No. 18 930 coming into effect, i.e. by 1 October 2012: *(i)* identification information; and *(ii)* the face value of the securities which they own (ss. 1 and 6 of Law No. 18 930). Where an issuing entity fails to provide the owner with a certificate within 30 days of submission of the information to the BCU (as described in the next point), the shareholder may file this information directly with the BCU (s. 6 of Law No. 18 930; s. 12 of Decree No. 247/012).
- Regardless of the shareholders' compliance with their reporting obligation above, the issuing entity must report this information (to the extent available), its total equity in par value and the equity interest of each owner to the BCU, through an affidavit, within 120 days of the effective date of Law No. 18 930, i.e. by 1 December 2012 (s. 6 of Law No. 18 930; s. 19 of Decree No. 247/012). Where an entity did not receive complete information from all shareholders, it was nevertheless required to fulfill its reporting obligation by filing a partially complete affidavit with the information that it possesse; however, an entity was not considered to have fulfilled its reporting obligation by filing a blank affidavit (s. 10 of Decree No. 247/012). An entity must issue a certificate to the relevant shareholder to evidence its reporting to the BCU. The entity must also retain the filed information for five years (s. 6 of Law No. 18 930).
- In relation to new issuance of bearer shares after the effective date of Law No. 18 930, owners must report to the issuing entity within 15 days from the issuance of the shares and the issuing entity will have 30 days from the expiry of that 15-day period to comply with its reporting obligations to the BCU (ss. 4 and 7 of Decree No. 247/012).
- A relevant entity must notify the BCU whenever its incorporation agreement is amended such that there is a change in the capital structure of the entity which alters the owners' percentage of total equity interest (s. 7 of Law No. 18 930; s. 8 of Decree No. 247/012).

- In relation to transfer of ownership, the new shareholder must notify the issuing entity within 15 days, providing his/her identity information, identity information relating to the transferor and also the date of transfer (s. 6 of Decree No. 247/012). The issuing entity must report this information to the BCU within 30 days of receipt of such information (s. 8 of Decree No. 247/012).
- The BCU maintains a register of the reported ownership information and issues certificates to evidence the registration status of issuing entities and natural persons under this reporting regime (s. 3 of Law No. 18 930). The register maintained by the BCU is available to the Uruguayan tax authorities, including for EOI purposes, subject to the provision of a resolution by the General Revenue Director (s. 5(a) of Law No. 18 930; s. 18 of Decree No. 247/012).

87. Decree No. 247/012 specifies a comprehensive list of identity information which must be provided by shareholders, in their affidavit to the issuing entity, in order to comply with their reporting obligations (s. 2 of Decree No. 247/012). In the case of natural persons this includes, amongst other things, the name of the owners, place of domicile, nationality, identity card number, foreign tax identification number issued by the Uruguayan tax authorities or identifying document issued by another jurisdiction, as appropriate. In the case of reporting shareholders which are legal persons, the information required includes: the name of the entity, the place and date of incorporation, its place of domicile, the consolidated taxpayers register number or foreign tax identification number issued by the Uruguayan tax authorities, as applicable. In each case, the extent of the information required is sufficient for the identification of the shareholder. Shareholders are required to inform the issuing entity of any change to the reported information within 15 days of the change, and the entity is in turn required to report this to the BCU within 30 day of receipt of the information (ss. 5 and 8 of Decree No. 247/012).

88. In the context of a transfer of shares, Law No. 18 930 imposes an obligation on the new owner to ensure that the transferor provides some certifiable evidence to demonstrate that he/she has fulfilled his/her reporting obligations with the BCU. A new owner which fails to do so will be held jointly and severally liable for the penalties imposed on the transferor, as a non-compliant owner (s. 10 of Law No. 18 930). The penalties may be determined up to 100 times the amount set out in Article 95 of the Tax Code. The fines set out in Article 95 of the Tax Code range from UYU 240 to UYU 5.640 (USD 10 to USD 235) for 2014 (USD 1: UYU 24).

89. Under the 2012 laws, failure by the new owner to comply with his/her obligation to request certifiable evidence from the transferor will not impede the transfer of share ownership from the transferor to the new owner in the

case where the transferor has complied with his/her own reporting obligation (pursuant to ss. 1 and 6 of Law No. 18 930). However, in such event, the new owner will become subject to the obligation to report to the issuing entity (ss. 1 and 6 of Law No. 18 930). In his/her notification to the issuing entity, the new owner must provide identifying information on the transferor as well as state the date of the transfer (s. 6 of Decree No. 247/012). Where the new owner fails to report his/her ownership and identification details to the issuing entity within 15 days of the transfer, he/she will be unable to exercise any rights as shareholder, whether as against the entity or a third party, until he/she has remedied the situation by complying with the reporting obligations and paid the relevant fine. (s. 6 of Decree No. 247/012; s. 8 of Law No. 18 930).

Consequences of non-compliance under the 2012 laws

90. Shareholders who have not complied with their reporting obligations to the issuing entity will be "unable to exercise any right to which they may be entitled as equity interest, in relation to the issuing entity or third parties" (s. 8(a) of Law No. 18 930). Uruguayan authorities had indicated that this entails that the ownership of shares cannot be legally transferred by the non-compliant shareholder to another person, although this is not explicitly so stated in the law. In addition, issuing entities cannot pay dividends, profits or capital from the winding up of the entity to non-compliant shareholders (s. 8(a) of Law No. 18 930). However, the Phase 1 supplementary report noted that these impediments to the exercise of shareholder rights may be removed once the non-compliant shareholder had fulfiled his/her reporting obligations, outside of the stipulated timeframe, and had paid the relevant fines which are further described below. It concluded accordingly that, the consequence of non compliance with the reporting obligations was a suspension (in addition to the relevant fines), but not a termination, of shareholder rights.

91. The Phase 1 supplementary report therefore noted that a gap remain under this reporting regime as regards ensuring that bearer shareholders could not remain undetected by the Uruguayan authorities for a potentially extended period of time, outside the stipulated timeframes for reporting described above. It also noted that this arose as result of the possibility of re-activation of the exercise of shareholder rights as described above, once the non-compliance with reporting obligations was rectified and accrued fines (as described below) were paid. Accordingly, a holder of a bearer share could, in effect, remain anonymous until the point where it was necessary to exercise his/her rights in the company. This could be a particular concern in relation to, non-trading, asset holding, closely held companies which did not regularly pay out dividends to their shareholders.

92. In addition, the report noted that as a result of the possibility of re-activation of shareholder rights, a gap could remain in practice under this

reporting regime as regards to ensuring that bearer shares could not continue to be transferred undetected by the Uruguayan authorities in some cases. Both in respect of existing bearer shares and new issuances, non-compliance with reporting obligations within the initial reporting period by the original bearer shareholder (i.e. by 1 October 2012 for existing bearer shareholdings, and within 15 days of the issuance of new bearer shares) resulted in the suspension in the exercise of his/her shareholder rights for the duration of their default. As noted above, Uruguay indicated that this means any transfer of ownership during such period would lack legal effect. However, this would not necessarily deter transferees from entering into such transfer arrangements in all cases, where it was known that the exercise of shareholder rights was merely suspended, and not terminated. However, it was noted that in such instance, the transferor would need to pay the accrued fine (described in section A.1.6) which could potentially be significant.

93. The report concluded that in these cases, it may be possible that ownership of bearer equity to be transferred, perhaps multiple times, without detection. A new owner may then report its ownership identification information to the issuing entity at a later date – for example, upon the declaration of dividend by the entity so as to safeguard their right to receive such payments and exercise their right as an equity holder. Although there is a separate obligation for the buyer (in his/her role as transferee) to report the change in ownership to the issuing entity (s. 6 of Decree No. 247/012), this does not necessarily eliminate the risk that where the original bearer shareholder (transferor) did not comply with his/her reporting obligations within relevant initial reporting period, that a transferee could simply report to the issuing entity outside of the specified period, as though remedying the original failure to report (as though he/she was an existing bearer shareholder during that initial reporting period) and thereby regain his/her ability to exercise full shareholder rights.

94. The report also noted that while the significant levels of fines which can be potentially imposed both in relation to shareholders and issuing entities should provide a strong deterrent in most cases against non compliance with the reporting obligations a concern remained with regard to how these penalties may be collected in practice, in particular in relation to non-compliant shareholders which are not resident or otherwise located in Uruguay. In addition, there were concerns as to the ability for the enforcement bodies to detect non-compliance with reporting obligations in the context of transfer of ownership or change in ownership details.

Mechanisms introduced by New Law 19 288

95. In response to the recommendation calling for Uruguay to clarify that effective enforcement provisions exist to support the requirements to

keep relevant ownership information in relation to all types of companies, Uruguay enacted further measures to address these concerns via Law 19 288 published to the Official Gazette on 17 October 2014. In addition, Law 19 288 adresses another significant gap in practice which emerged after Law 18 930 was enacted. This concerns the issue of non-compliant inactive bearer share companies. Thus Law 19 288 sets out two different sets of rules which apply during the initial 90-day period after the adoption of the Law, the first of which concerns inactive bearer share companies which do not comply with their reporting requirements and the second concerning non-compliant share-holders. These rules are described below.

96. As at 1 October 2014, there were approximately 75 000 inactive bearer companies which have not complied with the provisions of Law 18 930. In contrast, by May 8, 2014, the total number of active bearer share companies amounted to 37 596 of which 28 773 were fully compliant, such that 8 823 were non-compliant. Bearer share companies are considered inactive if they have been inactive for Uruguayan tax purposes. These are companies that were registered with the DGI but lost their status of active companies. This entails the following over a 3-year period: *(i)* the company did not record any tax payments, *(ii)* no payment received or paid by the company were subject to Uruguayan withholding tax; *(iii)* the company did not present any tax returns, *(iv)* the company did not request a business clearance certificate and *(v)* the company was not mentioned in any tax returns completed by the other taxpayers. The business clearance certificate of these inactive bearer share companies is already suspended, such that they cannot carry out business in Uruguay.

97. It is possible to have inactive bearer share companies with no assets, the shareholders of which are not actively carrying any activity through that company. In these cases, there would be no material gap in not having the identity of the bearer shareholders. However, although these companies are inactive for Uruguayan tax purposes, it may be possible that an inactive bearer share company holds assets abroad and/or receives foreign income which does not fall within the Uruguayan tax net due to Uruguay's territorial tax system. In such a case, the non-availability of ownership information of the non-compliant inactive bearer share company could potentially constitute a serious gap to the international standard.

98. The Uruguayan authorities stated that they realized there was a difficulty during the implementation of the 2012 Laws, and that they have actively worked on resolving the problem of inactive bearer share companies. They consider that Law 19 288 should remedy the situation by 30 May 2015 (see Section on Application Timeline of Law 19 288).

Rules applicable to the non-compliant bearer share companies

99. In addition to the reporting obligations set out in the 2012 laws, the following set of rules now apply to entities that have issued bearer shares:

- Any resident entities (defined in article 1 of the law 18 930) that have issued bearer shares, have 90 days from the effective date of the new law – that is from 1 November 2014 – to comply with the obligation to provide information regarding all the holders of bearer shares[11] by means of an affidavit representing 100% of the shareholding.
- Those entities that fail to report on ownership of bearer shares that represent at least 50% of the paid-up capital will be dissolved *ipso jure*, by the application of the law with effect from 29 January 2015. To determine the 50% threshold, the sum of bearer equity interests that are in compliance with the reporting obligations plus all nominative and book-entry equity interest shall be considered. The Uruguayan authorities clarified that the "50%-threshold" was chosen because it could be assumed that if the majority of the bearer shareholders are not identified, this would mean they do not wish for the company to continue, or are just unable to express their will for whatever reason (death etc.). In contrast, should the "50%-threshold" be met, this would demonstrate that the majority of the shareholders wish for the activities of the company to continue. In this case, the non-compliant bearer shareholders are subject to the other rules set out below. This rule shall not apply to bearer share entities whose shareholders have met their reporting obligations directly with the BCU. After the 90-day period – that is on 29 January 2015-, those companies failing to comply with the above-mentioned obligation will be terminated by operation of law and will have to be liquidated within 120 days from the end of the 90-day deadline[12]. This means that the deadline for liquidation will be 29 May 2015.
- For the purpose of the liquidation, the companies must hold an extraordinary meeting of shareholders in order to appoint a liquidator and to approve the initial inventory and balance sheet to liquidate the corporation. If no quorum is reached to hold the meeting or if the necessary majority is not reached, the balance sheet and the inventory shall be deemed to have been approved and the managers shall be in charge of liquidating the company. The person responsible for the liquidation will have to inform the DGI of the liquidation at the end of the liquidation process.[13]

11. Article 1 of Law 19 288.
12. Article 3 of Law 19 288.
13. Article 3 of Law 19 288.

- Entities, terminated by operation of Law, as of 29 January 2015, cannot be reactivated, which is a derogation from the domestic law normally applicable under Articles 165 and 166 of Law No 16.060).
- On 29 January 2015, the DGI will identify the companies to be dissolved and will communicate this information to the NRC and all the registries. Accordingly, in all administrative systems, there will be a red flag on the entities that are in a process of being liquidated.
- Once the 120-day term has expired – that is on 29 May 2015 – and no evidence of the due liquidation of the company has been given, the company will be subject to a fine equal to 50% of its assets, as determined by the Uruguayan valuation rules. Such fine will be collected by the AIN (article 4). This rule shall not apply if the ownership of the unreported bearer equity interests is subject to legal proceedings commenced before 29 January 2015 and as long as final judgment is not rendered.[14]
- The distribution of liquidation proceeds to the holders of the bearer equity interests in any of the entities issuing bearer shares, will be exempt from all taxes to the extent such distributions take place within the 120-day period (article 6).

100. All the above mentioned rules equally apply to all entities mentioned in article 1 of Law 19 830, i.e. associations, trusts and investment funds and any other entities that issue bearer shares (article 13).

Rules applicable to non-compliant shareholders

101. The second set of rules applies to the bearer shareholders and is as follows:

- Any bearer shareholders that do not file the affidavit as contemplated by the 2012 laws with the issuing entity within 90 days from the date of entry into force of law 19 288 – that is by 29 January 2015 – and who are shareholders of companies that have reported the ownership information of at least 50% of their capital, will individually lose their status as shareholders of the entity. The loss of shareholder status will take the form of a forced redemption/liquidation of their interest in the bearer share company. In this case, proceeds derived from the liquidated portion of equity will be distributed to the non-compliant shareholders. The bearer share entity will have to collect the fines applicable under the 2012 laws by deducting the amount of the fines from the distributable amount. The issuing entity shall

14. Article 12 of Law 19 288 and Article 8 of Decree 346/014 of 27 November 2014.

require prior to the payment the affidavit or the direct filing made by the bearer shareholder with the BCU. Failure to comply with this obligation will result in a fine equal to 50% of the amount which was unduly distributed to the non-compliant shareholder[15]. The issuing entity will be held severally liable for the amount of the fines. This mechanism applies as long as the companies are not liquidated pursuant to article 1 of the law.

102. The Uruguayan authorities have confirmed that the liquidation of the shareholder interests by the companies remains a private matter between the company and the shareholders, such that Law 19 288 does not prescribe any specific rules for the liquidation, but the general law on liquidation of shareholder's interest is applicable[16].

103. All the above mentioned rules equally apply to non-compliant shareholders of all entities mentioned in article 13 of Law 19 288, i.e. associations, trusts and investment funds and any other entities that issue bearer shares (article 14).

104. The Law also strengthens Law 18 930 by providing for a set of rules applicable after the 90-day period – that is on 29 January 2015:

- From that date, the BCU shall only accept filings containing information of 100% of the issued participations. If the entities do not comply with this provision, the AIN will apply the penalties set out in Article 8 and 9 of law No 18.930 (Article 16 a) of Law 19 288).
- For all entities subject to the 2012 laws that have issued bearer shares, a general presumption will be applicable under which the shareholders will be deemed to be the founders or the last recorded shareholders of the entities, in case the holders of the bearer shares issued by such entities do not comply with their identification requirements (Article 16 b) of Law 19 288. This means that the founders or predecessors are subject to the penalties under the 2012 laws if they fail to ensure the registration of the new shareholders.
- The bearer share holder will lose his/her status as shareholder as set out in article 12 and article 14 of the law, in case the bylaws or equivalent are changed or the percentage of ownership is modified pursuant to capital increase, or in the case of a transfer of shares[17] and the bearer share holder does not comply with the reporting obligation to the BCU pursuant to the reporting requirements under the 2012 Laws (Article 16 c) of Law 19 288). The loss of status will take

15. Article 12 of Law 19 288.
16. Articles 154 and 155 of Law 16 060.
17. Article 16c) of Law 19 288.

place after a 90-day period has elapsed after the deadline imposed by the 2012 Laws. This entails that the issuing company will redeem the interest held by the non-compliant shareholder. From the proceeds distributed to the non-compliant shareholder, the issuing entity will have to collect the fines applicable under the 2012 Laws and pay the amount to the AIN.

105. After 29 January 2015, any newly-established entities will be subject to the standard reporting requirements and sanctions as set out in the 2012 Laws. The non-compliance by the newly-established entities with their reporting requirements within 15 days of incorporation will be detected almost instantly by the BCU, which will inform the AIN and the DGI. As such, the non-compliant newly established entities will lose their clearance business certificate with the DGI and will be unable to carry out business activities in Uruguay. In addition, the AIN will impose the fines on the non-compliant entity as set out under the 2012 Laws. Furthermore, the non-compliant shareholders will lose their status as shareholders as set out in Article 16 c) of Law 19 288.

Conclusion on effectiveness of new Law 19 288 to cover the gaps identified in the Phase 1 supplementary report

106. The mechanisms introduced by Law 19 288 should allow the ownership identification of all bearer shares in circulation in Uruguay, as this targets both non-compliant entities and non-compliant shareholders. The Phase 1 supplementary report identified a possible gap under the 2012 laws regarding the possibility for the bearer shares to be transferred without detection. Law 19 288 addresses this concern by replacing the penalty of suspension of the shareholder's right by an extinction of such shareholder's right. The non-compliant shareholder which fails to comply with its reporting requirement will lose its shareholder status and will receive the proceeds of the liquidation of its equity rights. In addition, the presumption that the actual holders shall be the founders or the last registered shareholders of the bearer shares will provide an incentive for former shareholders to declare they are no longer the shareholders, because they will want to avoid being severally liable for non-compliance. As a result, non-compliance by the new shareholder will be more easily detected. This presumption will also constitute an incentive for the new bearer share holder to comply with his registration requirements, as the new shareholder will not want that the economic and voting rights attached to the shares remain in the hand of the previous shareholder.

Monitoring of the relevant laws in practice

107. As law 19 288 entered into force on 1 November 2014, it is currently being implemented, and there has been no opportunity yet to monitor the

changes which it introduced. However, significant steps were taken by Uruguay to effectively to implement and monitor the 2012 laws.

108. For the purpose of implementing and monitoring those laws, a team of seven persons was constituted within the Internal Audit Department (*Auditoria Internal de la Nación* (AIN)). The team, which started the implementation work in April 2012, is composed of accountants, lawyers and notaries. AIN is a public body created in 1989[18] that has technical autonomy from the executive branch. AIN has a public website[19], which provides access since November 2012 to all information related to Law 18930. Since 1 August 2013, a special Commission within the AIN (*Comisión Fiscalizadora de Participaciones Patrimoniales*) was established for the purposes of monitoring the application of law 18930.

109. Under article 4 of Law 18 930, AIN's mission entails *(i)* carrying out compliance control of the obligations set forth in Law 18 930, *(ii)* communicating incidents of non-compliance to the appropriate Uruguayan authorities, *(iii)* imposing and collecting pecuniary penalties as set out in Article 11 of law 18 930 and *(iv)* receiving the non-compliance claims from, amongst others, the DGI. The AIN is authorised to request from the DGI and the BCU specific information to define the level of penalties, or any relevant information relevant to comply with its mission. The AIN is also granted authority to require from companies any information required to accomplish its mission. The AIN is subject to confidentiality obligations[20]. Guidelines have been adopted regarding the treatment of the information for confidentiality purposes.

110. In substance, Law 18 930 establishes two options for companies that have issued bearer shares:

- To convert the bearer shares into nominative shares; or
- To comply with the bearer share holder identification requirements with the BCU.

Conversion of the bearer shares into nominative shares

111. Article 17 of Law 18 930 sets out a specific regime for corporations converting their share capital in bearer shares into nominative shares. To implement article 17 of Law 18930 in practice, the AIN established a specific procedure by means of a Decree and a Guideline. Following the entry into force of Law 18 930, the AIN had to deal with a large flow of bearer

18. AIN was created by the Business Partnerships Law (*Ley de Sociedades Comerciales n° 16.060 de 1989*).
19. www.ain.gub.uy/.
20. Article 5 of Law 18930.

shares companies converting their share capital into nominative shares. As of 24 July 2014, 10 539 companies had converted their bearer share capital into nominative shares.

112. Under this special procedure, companies must first register the conversion of their share capital with the NRC, which in turn publishes a notice in the Official Gazette. Subsequently, these companies have 60 days and 30 days to inform the AIN and the DGI to record the modification, respectively. Decree 597/988 set out the penalties in case the companies fails to register. In practice, more than 2 000 fines have been imposed during the peer review period[21] when bearer share companies converted their shares in nominative shares. The fines were imposed due to the non-compliance by some of the converted companies with the filing requirements set out in Law 18 930 and applicable since October 2012. As a matter of procedure, the DGI automatically makes the change in its records. After the peer review period, the Taxpayer Assistance and Guidance Division have launched a public campaign in order to improve compliance.

Identification requirements with the BCU

113. The AIN is in charge of monitoring the compliance by bearer share companies with the identification requirements. For this purposes, the AIN first had to establish the monitoring mechanisms. Since early 2012, the AIN interacted with the DGI, BCU and NRC to establish a working framework. The AIN concluded Memorandum of Understandings with the BCU and the DGI to allow for exchange of information between those authorities. The AIN also carried out training activities with the association of accountants, the association of notaries, and also internally for building awareness of the new framework.

114. The AIN together with the BCU prepared forms for the registration of bearer shareholders. Form A is the one with which bearer the shareholder informs the company about its ownership identity. Form B is the one used by the bearer share companies to inform the BCU. Sanctions for failure to comply with the registration requirements are set out in Section A.1.6 *Enforcement provisions to ensure availability of information*, and include *inter alia* loss of business certificates for non-compliant companies, fines and loss of shareholder's status for non-compliant shareholders. In a few instances, the bearer shareholder informed the BCU directly of its identity. In these cases, the bearer share company had failed to inform the BCU before the expiry of the term. But the bearer shareholder was entitled to inform the BCU directly, as foreseen in Form B and Article 12 of Decree 247/012.

21. Under Section 95 of the Tax Code, violation of laws or regulations passed by "the corresponding bodies that determine formal duties" is punishable by a fine ranging from UYU 240 to UYU 5.640 (USD 10 to USD 235) for 2014 (ESD 1: UYU 24).

Impact of Law 18 930 on the issuance of bearer shares

115. Law 18 930 appears to have had an impact on the issuance of bearer shares since its adoption in 2012. The number of newly-incorporated bearer share companies has dropped by about 60% in 2012 and 2013, as compared to the numbers of 2010 and 2011.

The table below provides the number of newly-incorporated bearer share companies per year, which have registered with the DGI (i.e. active bearer share companies).

Year	2010	2011	2012	2013*
Number of new bearer share companies	2 490	2 611	1 074	985

* For reference purposes, the number decreased to 361 as at 18 November 2014.

116. The total number of active bearer share companies over the peer review period is the following:

Year	2010	2011	2012	2013 (31 dec)
Number of active bearer share companies	55 612	54 267	53 048	43 973*

* As of May 8th 2014, the total amount of active bearer share companies amounted to 37 596.

Application timeline of Law 19 288

117. Law 19 288 was published in the Official Gazette on 17 October 2014 and entered into force on 1 November 2014. From that date, the 90-day period to comply with the rules of the 2012 Laws started to run with a deadline as at 29 January 2015 both for non-compliant entities and for non-compliant shareholders.

118. For awareness building on the provisions of Law 19 288, the DGI organised a media campaign "the last chance" which took place in the national newspapers, in conjunction with lawyers, notaries and accounting to inform the public about the rules and deadlines set out in Law 19 288 and to improve the compliance rate. Decree 346/014 implementing Law 19 288 issued on 27 November 2014 published the list of inactive bearer share companies in the Official Gazette, with the aim to inform them about their obligations and provide them with the opportunity to come forward to correct any mistake in the list.

119. On 29 January 2015, after the end of the 90-day period, the DGI will identify the entities dissolved by effect of the law in its RUT and will communicate this information to all the relevant Uruguayan authorities – that is the *Banco de Prevision Social* (BPS) and the *Direccion General de Registros* (including the NRC) of these entities – such that these entities will be red flagged.

120. These non-compliant entities, subject to the 50%-threshold rule described in Section A.1.2 *bearer shares*, and which will be dissolved by 29 January 2015 by effect of the law, will have 120 days to liquidate. This 120-day period will end on 29 May 2015. Companies having identified the owners of more than 50% of the capital but less than 100% will have to redeem the shares of non-compliant bearer shareholders and deduct the pecuniary fines from the redemption payment paid to the non-compliant shareholders, as set out section A.1.2 *Bearer Shares*.

Conclusion on effective implementation of the 2012 laws and Law 19 288

121. As set out above, Uruguay has taken significant steps to implement and monitor the 2012 laws, and furthermore to frame new legal measures to address the shortcomings identified in practice in respect of inactive bearer shares and in the Phase 1 Supplementary report. Uruguay has already put in place the implementation framework of Law 19 288. Ownership and identity information on bearer shares is ensured through the application of multiple obligations:

- As of 29 January 2015, all non-compliant inactive bearer share companies will be dissolved by law and the final deadline for liquidation of the non-compliant inactive bearer share companies will take place as at 29 May 2015.
- Regarding ownership transfers, the new bearer shareholder must inform the issuing entity within 15 days following the share purchase and provide this entity all identifying information. Failure to comply with this requirement results in the pecuniary fines set out Articles 8 & 9 of Law 18 930. In addition, pursuant to Article 16 c) of Law 19 288, if the new shareholder does not comply with the obligation within 90 days after the initial 15-day registration period has elapsed, his shareholder's interest will be redeemed and a pecuniary sanction will be deducted from the redemption payment. These loss of shareholder's rights and the effective application of pecuniary penalties, which are deducted from the redemption payment, should constitute a strong incentive for any new shareholders to comply with their reporting requirements.

122. However, the changes introduced in Law 19 288 are very recent and have not been tested in practice. Therefore it is recommended that Uruguay should continue to devote the significant resources which it has already assembled to ensure that the provision of Law 19 288 are effectively implemented and monitored.

Information requests received on bearer shares during the peer review period

123. During the period under review, Uruguay received four information requests dealing with bearer share companies, three of which concerned VAT cases and fall out of the scope of this review.

124. The remaining request was received before the Law 18 930 came into effect. The request dealt with ownership information of a bearer share company. The DGI asked the company for the ownership information on the bearer shareholders, which in turn provided the information. Hence, the information was available and provided to the peer within 96 days. The peer was satisfied with the information provided by Uruguay.

Partnerships *(ToR A.1.3)*

125. As noted in section A.1.1, all commercial entities in Uruguay are "business partnerships" which in addition to the forms described in the Companies section of the report, may take one of the other forms described in the Business Partnerships Law (article 3) including the following types of partnerships:

i. General Partnership (*Sociedades Colectivas* (SC), Ch II, Sect. I, article 199): the members are jointly and severally liable without limit (that is, this type of entity is similar to a common law partnership, rather than a company with a separate legal identity). As of 30 June 2014, there were 444 SCs registered with the DGI.

4. Limited Partnerships (*Sociedades en Comandita Simple* (SCS), Ch II Sect. II, article 212): partnership shares divided between the active partner(s), who has unlimited liability; and special partner(s), who is liable only to the extent of their contribution. Subject to the express provisions of chapter II, section II of the Business Partnerships Law, the regulations regarding general partnerships are applicable to limited partnerships. As of 30 June 2014, there were 116 active SCS registered with the the DGI.

ii. Capital and Labour Partnerships (*Sociedades de capital e industria),* Ch II, Sect. III, article 218): partnership shares are divided between funding partners, who have unlimited liability; and working partners, who only contribute their labour and are liable only up to the amount of profits due to them which they have not received. Subject to the express provisions of chapter II, section III of the Business Partnerships

Law, the regulations applying to general partnerships are applicable to Capital and Labour Partnerships. As of 30 June 2014, there were 5 *Sociedades de capital e industria*, registered with the DGI.

126. Article 6 of the Business Partnerships Law provides that a deed constituting all types of business partnerships will be made and must contain certain information including the name and address of the business partnership and accurate identification of those entering into the contract (i.e. the founding members) and their capital contributions. As with companies, a partnership's founding document must be registered in the NRC within 30 days (article 7). Article 49 of the Public Register Law 16 871 also provides for registration in the NCR of all deeds of incorporation for commercial partnerships.

127. With respect to the registration in the NRC of the transfer of ownership parts, Uruguay has advised that as this is considered a modification of the incorporation contract, such transfers must also be notified to the NRC pursuant to article 10 of the Business Partnerships Law[22]. Similarly, article 49(10) of the Public Register Law requires the notification of the NRC of any modifications to the incorporation contract, which includes identity information on the partners (whether limited or otherwise).

128. In addition for general partnerships, the partnership itself is subject to an implied obligation to keep a record of transfers of ownership parts. Article 211 of the Business Partnerships Law provides that an assignment of a part to another partner or a third party shall only occur by unanimous consent (although though there is no express requirement for the general partnership itself to keep a record of such consent or the subsequent transfer).

129. Partnerships are taxed at the partnership level in Uruguay, and all partnerships formed under the Business Partnerships Law are subject to tax in Uruguay. All entities, including partnerships are required to register with the DGI at the time of starting or restarting taxable activity, providing to the DGI the "information and documents that are required" (article 9, Decree 597/988). Uruguay has advised that this will include the provision of certain information, which must be kept up to date, including the partnership's full name and business address, although not complete ownership information. Article 63 of the Tax Code requires that in a tax return, a taxpayer must provide "all elements and background information" required by laws and regulations which are necessary for a tax determination, and Uruguay has

22. As mentioned in respect of companies, it is not clear that notification of transfers to the NRC results in the maintenance of a complete share register by the NRC, or whether alternatively, each of the transfers is merely filed in the entity's file maintained by the NRC.

advised that on this basis, the partnership will provide identity information regarding the partners. However, noting that partnerships are taxed at the partnership level, it does not appear that this is clearly established by article 63 of the Tax Code.

130. In addition, section 22 of Law No. 18 930 sets out a new requirement for the registration of sale of stakeholdings in partnerships with the DGI prior to registration of such transfer with the General Registries Office which controls the NRC. This is supplemented by Decree No. 247/012 which provides that registration of such sale and assignment with the DGI must occurs within 30 days of the contract of sale or assignment (s. 1 of Decree No. 242/012, inserting s. 30(bis) in Decree No. 597/988). This new registration requirement is supported by enforcement provisions under the Tax Code (see A.1.6 below).

131. In sum therefore, all types of partnerships formed under the Business Partnerships Law are subject to requirements under that law, the tax laws and the NRC Law that will ensure that the identity of the partners is known. All the observations and conclusions applicable to foreign companies are equally applicable to foreign partnerships.

132. As at 30 June 2014, there were with 512 General Partnerships, 125 Limited Partnerships, and 7 Capital and Labour Partnerships.

133. In practice, the registration of partnerships is performed in the same way as the registration of companies and the information on partnerships is maintained with the NRC. Partnerships must have a RUT number. Two EOI requests were received concerning ownership information about Uruguayan partnerships, but dealt with VAT matters. Although this information was available and obtained from the taxpayer in a timely manner, as has been the treatment of VAT requests to date these two requests are not counted for the purpose of this report.

Trusts *(ToR A.1.4)*

134. The statutory provisions relating to the creation and governance of trusts (*fideicomisos*) in Uruguay are contained in Law 17 703 published on 4 November 2003 (Trusts Law) and Decree No. 516/003 (Trusts Decree), as amended by Decrees Nos. 46/004 and 52/004. As of 30 June 2014, there were 298 *fideicomisos* registered with the DGI.

135. Article 1 of the Trusts Law defines a trust as a juridical act whereby the fiduciary ownership of a group of property rights or other rights is created and transferred by the settlor (*fideicomitente*) to the trustee (*fiduciario*).

136. Pursuant to Article 2 of the Trusts Law, a trust can be created *inter vivos* or by an open or closed will. Express trusts must be established in writing. An express trust may be either:

- *non-financial trust*: established through the creation of a trust agreement between the settlor and the trustee. A *guarantee trust (fideicomiso de garantía)* is a sub-type of non-financial trust which is created for the purpose of allowing a debtor to transfer immovable or movable property into the trust, to guarantee the payment of their debt which is outstanding.; or
- *financial trust (fideicomiso financiero)*: akin to a unit trust,[23] and which may be established by the unilateral act of a financial intermediary or an entity managing investment funds. Subject to the specific provisions of chapter IV of the Trusts Law.

Non-financial trusts (including guarantee trusts)

137. The trust instrument as a contract must be authorised by a public notary. Under article 130 of the Supreme Court of Justice's regulations governing public notaries (Acordada no. 7 533), all deeds must contain certain identity information including the full name and nationality and address of the parties involved. The beneficiary must be designated in the trust deed (article 23, Trusts Law). Where the trust deed names a class of beneficiaries some of whom are not yet in existence, the law requires that the means allowing for their future identification are described in the trust instrument (article 23, Trusts Law).Therefore, the identity of the settlor, trustee and beneficiary will be known in respect of all trusts created under Uruguay's law.

138. Further, the trust instrument, and any modification or cancellation thereof, must be registered in the Private Acts Registry within the Properties Section of the Ministry of Education and Culture (art 6, Trusts Law; s. 1, Trusts Decree), and only becomes enforceable against third parties upon registration (art. 17, Trusts Law). For the registration to be admitted the trust instrument must indicate identity information for trustees (s2, Trusts Decree). This identity information includes:

- for individuals, full name, address and identity card number; or
- for legal entities, name, type, registered office address and registration number.

139. Foreign-administered trusts created under Uruguayan law, will also be subject to the requirements described above.

23. Article 25, Trusts Law, defines a financial trust as a "trust whose beneficiaries are holders of beneficial ownership certificates or debt securities guaranteed by assets held in trust or of mixed securities granting credit rights over and interests in the remainder.

Financial trusts

140. A financial trust, governed by articles 25 to 32 of the Trusts Law, may be established by a financial intermediary or an entity managing investment funds. As for non-financial trusts, the trust must be registered in the Private Acts Registry and in order to be registered a financial trust instrument must indicate identity information for trustees and for settlors (s2, Trusts Decree). Where the settlor and the trustee are the same person, the trust may be established through a unilateral act (articles 25 and 26, Trusts Law). Financial trusts may make public or private offerings of securities, with the latter being required to register with the BCU (art 3, Law 16 749; and s. 13, Trusts Decree). Financial trusts are required to report to the BCU any change in their deed pursuant to article 108(1) of the Securities Market Rules.

141. All trust deeds created under Uruguayan law must be notarised by a public notary and must include the full name, nationality and address of the parties to the deed. Therefore, the identity of the settlor, trustee and beneficiary will be known in respect of all trusts, including financial trusts, created under Uruguay's law.

Trustees

142. For tax purposes, a trust (except for guarantee trusts) is a taxable entity (article 36, Trusts Law) however it is the trustee who is the "tax responsible" party (article 44, Trusts Law, with articles 16 and 19 of the Tax Code). Accordingly, the trustee is responsible for ensuring that the trust meets its obligations under the tax laws, such as registration of the trust with the DGI, the filing of tax returns and the payment of any taxes due. The trustee shall be personally responsible for meeting those obligations (article 44, Trusts Law), that is, he may be required to pay outstanding taxes from the trustee's own assets if there are insufficient assets held in the trust.[24]

143. Under article 11 of the Trusts Law, any natural person with the legal capacity required to perform commercial activities or any legal person may be a trustee. Uruguay has advised that regulations issued by the BCU distinguish between the following types of trustees (Trusts Law, article 11; and Trusts Decree, section 11):

- *general trustee*: establishes non-financial trusts on a non-regular basis;

24. In the case of a guarantee trust, for tax purposes the assets of the trust are still considered assets of the settlor (article 58, Law 18 083).

- *professional trustee*: acts on a regular basis, in a professional capacity, where regular basis means establishing five or more non-financial trusts in a given calendar year; and
- *financial trustee*: a sub-type of professional trustee, being a financial intermediary or entity managing investment funds which establishes financial trusts (regardless of the number of financial trusts established in a given year).

Professional trustees

144. Professional (including financial) trustees are subject to a requirement to register in the Public Registry of Professional Trustees kept by the BCU (Trusts Law, article 12 and Trusts Decree, section 6). On 18 November 2014, there were 14 professional trustees registered with the BCU. Such trustees who are not individuals must disclose their own ownership information (shareholders, partners, managers and directors) and accounting information (last three business years) to the BCU, as part of the registration process (Trusts Law, article 12 and Trusts Decree, sections 7 and 8). Further, if a corporation is appointed to act as a trustee, it may issue only issue nominative or book-entry shares (Trusts Law, article 12). Further, all professional trustees are carrying out "financial intermediation" activities and therefore will be subject to the regulations described in section A.3.1 and the AML regime. Those obligations mean that where the trust is managed by a professional trustee, the identity of the settlor will be known, and at the time of the distribution of funds from the trust, the professional trustee will also need to identify the beneficiary.

145. In addition, financial trustees must submit the articles of incorporation of their financial trusts and expressly indicate whether they will issue public or private offerings of securities (Trusts Decree, sections 11 and 12). This information is publicly available and must be updated at least on a half-yearly basis (Trusts Law, article 12 and Trusts Decree, section 15).

146. Therefore, for trusts managed by professional trustees (but not created under Uruguayan law) the identity information relating to the trustee and settlor will be available, as well as the beneficiaries at the time of distribution of funds. In practice, the tax administration has never come across the situation of a Uruguayan trustee of a foreign trust, either in its domestic work or in relation to exchange of information. A very narrow gap potentially remains in relation to those trusts administered in Uruguay, but not created under Uruguayan law, which have a non-professional trustee. The Uruguayan authorities have clarified that they are not aware of individuals carrying out trustees functions in a non-professional capacity in Uruguay. However, the Uruguayan authorities have confirmed they stand ready to answer any incoming requests received in relation to these arrangements. The position of

trustees acting in a non-business capacity (and therefore not be covered by the AML/CFT requirements) and the effect on EOI in practice should continue to be monitored by Uruguay to ensure that identity information is made available in all cases.

147. Non-resident trustees of trusts with Uruguayan assets are required to register with the BCU and to submit a proof of their registration, if any, with a relevant trust authority in their country of residence (Trusts Decree, section 9). As at 18 November 2014, there were no non-resident trustees registered with the BCU.

148. For trusts created under Uruguayan law, whether non-financial trusts (including guarantee trusts) or financial, the trustee settlor and beneficiaries will be identified.

149. Uruguay has not received any requests regarding trusts during the peer review period.

Foundations (ToR A.1.5)

150. Uruguay has advised that foundations can be created under Uruguayan law, pursuant to the Foundation Law 17 163 but they must be not for-profit. Therefore and to that extent, they are of limited pertinence to the exchange of information for tax purposes; however a brief overview of their legal structure, and ownership and identity information requirements is given here. As of 30 June 2014, foundations registered with the NRC amounted to 688 foundations.

151. Under Uruguayan, law, a foundation will have both a managing council and an administrative council, and the degree of control over the assets of the foundation by each body is not known. The foundation's articles of incorporation must contain the identity of its founding members. The foundation must be registered with the Civil Association Agency (part of the Ministry of Culture and Education.) including the articles of incorporation, and information including the foundation name and address, its purpose, initial capital, and the names of the members of the managing council. Members of the managing council, and any managers of the foundation, are required to reside in Uruguay. After liquidation, any assets remaining may only be donated to another not for profit organisation with similar activities or aim; or the assets become the property of the Minister of Culture and Education.

152. A Uruguayan foundation is exempt from tax to the extent of its non-profit activities, and therefore is not generally required to either file a tax return. However, to the extent that it undertakes activities which are not strictly linked to their non-profit purpose to which their tax-exempt status is linked, they are liable to pay tax.

153. Uruguay has not received any requests regarding foundations during the peer review period.

Other types of legal entities and arrangements

154. In addition to companies and partnerships, certain other types of "business partnerships" may be created under the Commerce Law, namely:

(i) Informal Partnership or Joint Ventures (*Sociedades Accidentales o en participación,* Ch II, Sect. VII, article 483): A contract amongst two or more people whose aim is to perform certain temporary business, where the contract is executed under the name of one or more managers. It does not create a legal personality, and are not subject to any formal or registration requirements. Any third parties shall only acquire rights and assume obligations in relation to the manager, whose liability is limited.

(ii) Economic Interest Groups (*Grupos de Interés Económico,* Ch III, Sect I, article 489) A contract arranged between two or more persons or entities in order to develop or facilitate the economic activity of its members. It is not allowed to collect or distribute profits. The contract should contain the management and representation rules otherwise the rules applying to corporations will be applied. In other matters General Partnerships regulations will apply. Partners may have a jointly and several, or subsidiary liability depending on the terms of the contract. It is a legal entity, and recognised as taxpayer by Article 9 of Law 18.083. Its contract of incorporation, which includes ownership information, and any modifications to it, must be registered in the NRC. Its shares cannot be transferred.

(iii) Consortium or Association (*Consorcios*, Ch III, Sect II, article 501): A contract arranged between two or more persons or entities in order to develop temporarily some labour, services or goods supplement. Its purpose is not to collect and distribute profits, but to regulate the activity to be carried out. It will be managed by one or more administrator. The rules applying to general partnership will be applicable. It does not create a separate legal personality, but its constitutional contract, which includes ownership information, and any modifications must be registered and published in the NRC.

155. Each of the above types of "business partnerships" are subject to the same requirements as companies and partnerships to register their deeds of incorporation with the NRC, and to notify the NRC of any modifications of those documents, including relevantly, any change to the involved parties (articles 6, 7 and 10 of the NRC Law). These provisions ensure that ownership

and identity information will be available for each of these types of "business partnership".

156. In practice, Uruguay has not received an EOI request about these entities during the peer review period.

157. In addition, there are some other types of arrangements which can be formed under Uruguayan law, relevantly investment funds and offshore financial institutions.

Investment Funds

158. In Uruguay, investment funds are not considered as companies or other type of separate legal entities. The assets are owned by the investors and managed by a corporation with shareholders, directors, managers and high executives staff who are identified and have the obligation to inform BCU of all changes or transferences. Whilst they are not legal entities, certain types of investment funds (closed investment funds) are deemed to be taxpayers in their own right (article 9, Law 18 083).

159. Investment funds may be open funds, closed funds,[25] or pension funds. Open and closed investment funds are regulated by Laws 16 774, 17 202, whilst pension funds are regulated under Law 16 713. All investment funds (including pension funds) are subject to supervision by the BCU. Funds must be managed by a corporation[26] who will be considered to be carrying out "financial intermediation" and subject to the regulations described in Section A.3.1 under the supervision of the BCU. Investments in a fund are represented by securities called "cuotapartes" (shares) which may be issued as nominative, bearer or book-entry shares (article 4, Law 16 774). Pension funds are only allowed to issue nominative shares.

160. In respect of bearer shares issued by investment funds, a new Stock Market Law 18 627 passed in 2009 provides that all values listed in the market must be electronic and nominative. While this law does not expressly provide that investment funds may not issue bearer shares, Uruguay has advised that under the "latter in time" principle of hierarchy of laws, it will abrograte Laws 16 774 and 17 202 to the extent they permitted the issuance of bearer shares by investment funds. The Stock Market Law does not appear to address closed investment funds which are not required to be listed on the

25. Closed investment funds are established for the purpose relating to assigned credit rights. Investors assign credit rights to the managing corporation (such credit rights must stem from the investor's ordinary business) and the managing company acts effectively as a broker to third parties to factor those rights.
26. Shares in the managing corporation itself may only be issued in nominative or book-entry form.

stock market, or otherwise provide a mechanism to identify any bearer shares that it may have been issued.

161. For all types of funds, the managing corporation must keep an up to date register of shares in the fund (open and closed funds: articles 10, 14, and 25, Law 16 774; pension funds: article 86, Law 16 713), and in the case of nominative and book-entry shares this will include identity information of the investors. The managing corporation may appoint another person to keep the register of shares (section 4, Law16 774) although that person will also be considered to be carrying out financial intermediation activities and be subject to regulation.

162. All investment funds operating in Uruguay listed on a public market are bound to issue book entry shares. Private investment fund can issue "bearer shares" "nominative shares" or "book entry shares" (article 4 Law 16.774). Private investment funds issuing bearer shares must comply with the reporting requirements set out Law 18.930, even if the investment funds are open-ended or closed-ended. As at 1 October 2014, no private investment funds were registered with the BCU. The authorities of Uruguay have clarified that the BCU would not authorize the registration of an investment fund that has issued bearer shares, because such investment fund would not fulfill the obligations under AML legislation.

Offshore Financial Institutions

163. Offshore Financial Institutions (IFEs) are not a separate type of legal form, but a classification for entities whose only purpose consists of carrying out intermediation activities regarding the offer and demand of securities, money or precious metals located abroad. They may take various legal forms, including being a branch of a public or private foreign bank, a corporation (where that corporation has issued only nominative shares that must be owned by a bank), or a physical person with experience in the international financial field and approved by the BCU. The IFE must follow the registration requirements applicable to their particular legal form. This includes, where they operate as a branch of a foreign bank and carry out activities in Uruguay, they must satisfy the requirements for foreign companies described in Section A.1.1 (*foreign companies*). They will also be subject to regulation by the BCU and the Financial Intermediary Institution Commission (SIIF) and subject to the obligations for all persons carrying out financial intermediation activities as described in Section A.1.3.

164. In practice, Uruguay did not receive an EOI request about IFEs during the peer review period.

Enforcement provisions to ensure availability of information (ToR A.1.6)

Domestic companies

165. A company will be liable for any damages caused to third parties as a result of the failure to file the necessary records in the NRC or meet the record-keeping obligations of the Business Partnerships Law, for example stemming from the unenforceability of a contract (article 54, Business Partnerships Law). Personal liability is imposed severally on directors of the company in respect of such damages (article 39, Business Partnerships Law). Also, neither the company nor its members may rely on the documents incorporating the company as against third parties (article 37, Business Partnerships Law) and third parties may file proceedings for damages jointly or severally against the company, its partners or managers (article 39, Business Partnerships Law). Only companies carrying on certain activities (media and public carrier companies) are subject to an express requirement to have company directors either reside in Uruguay or be Uruguayan citizens.

166. Specific sanctions are provided in respect of corporations when they violate any applicable law, statute or regulation. Article 412 of the Business Partnerships Law provides that the supervisory body may impose measures on the corporation itself, or its officers, directors or managers, in the form of a written warning (which will be published), or a fine of up to UYU 1 000. Failure to keep a share register is monitored by the tax authorities at the occasion of tax audits carried out at the premises of the corporations (see A.2 *Availability of Accounting information*).

167. A gap was identified in the Phase 1 supplementary report in relation to clarification of enforcement provisions which apply to support provisions to ensure that ownership information is available in relation to the formation of Uruguayan companies (which are neither corporations nor issue bearer shares) and partnerships, as opposed to upon subsequent transfers. In this respect, officials from the DGI have advised that in the case of companies (which are neither corporations nor issue bearer shares; that is in the case of limited liability companies (SRLs)) and partnerships (hereinafter called personal companies), these personal companies must firstly go to the public notary in order to be constituted (article 88 and 89 Law N° 16871). In the case that the constitution is not registered with the public notary, the personal company does not exist for legal purposes and cannot be registered with the NRC, nor can it obtain a Tax Identification Number in the RUT at the DGI. No enforcement measures to ensure that ownership information are necessary in these cases because, if the formalities with the public notary are not duly carried out, the personal company will not have any legal existence (see Section A.1.1 *Ownership and identity information on Companies*). Hence, if

the personal company is duly constituted, the information on the ownership information of the founders of personal companies is available with the public notary, which is subject to AML rules and Customer Due Diligence obligations, with the DGI (where the bylaws are registered) and with the NRC.

Foreign companies

168. Foreign companies failing to report to the identity of their owners within 120 days of the effective date of Law No. 18 930, i.e. by 1 December 2012, and all subsequent changes in ownership to the BCU within 30 days of receipt of such information are subject to a range of sanctions: administrative fines apply to both the non-compliant entities and to their representatives (to the extent of their culpability). The amount of fines which may be applied depends upon the size of the issuing entity, their relative participation in such entity and the length of time for which they have held the shares and ranges from approximately UYU 10 000 to UYU 500 000 (approximately USD 250 to USD 25 000, ss. 8 and 9 of Law No. 18 930 and s. 17 of Decree No. 247/012). In addition, a non compliant entity may have its certificate discontinued by the General Taxation Office and be denied the right to register their legal acts in the registers maintained by the General Registries Office, both of which are necessary for the conduct of business and/or holding of assets in Uruguay (s. 12 of Law No. 18 930 and art. 80 of title 1 of the Amended 1996 Text; s. 14 of Decree No. 247/012).

169. In practice, the reporting requirements on ownership of foreign companies are supported by a range of sanctions which apply to non-compliant foreign companies. Administrative penalties apply to both the non-compliant foreign companies and to their legal representatives in Uruguay. The monitoring mechanism put in place is part of that implemented for bearer shares (see below). As of June 2014, the BCU and the AIN have compiled a list of 525 foreign companies with sufficient nexus in Uruguay which had not submitted the affidavits regarding the identity of their shareholders. As at 1 June 2014, the AIN had issued 486 administrative penalties for failure to comply with ownership recording obligations.

170. Another sanction, which was immediate, consisted in the suspension of their clearance certificate by the DGI (Art 15 of Law 18930) for all 525 foreign companies. Without such clearance certificate, companies, being domestic or foreign, cannot carry out any activities in Uruguay. The consequences are, amongst other things, that the companies cannot issue and print invoices, they cannot participate in legal tenders, they cannot ask for any loans in the financial sector, nor import, export or render services to the government. The pecuniary penalties are applied by the AIN (Article 4(c) of the law 18930). The AIN work from a list determined by the DGI and then determines the level of penalties, depending on the size of the infringing entity.

171. Although the compliance percentage was low at the end of the peer review period, the monitoring plan carried out by the DGI, in collaboration with the AIN, which started towards the end of the peer review period, ensures a total coverage of foreign companies operating in Uruguay and not just those that have a tax residence in Uruguay. Moreover, the monitoring plan provides for the application of strict sanctions applicable to non-compliant foreign companies. It shall be noted that the number of foreign companies is minimal in comparison with the amount of domestic companies in Uruguay. As a result of these elements, the materiality of the gap in practice is minimal. Nevertheless, Uruguay should continue to monitor the compliance by foreign companies with the provisions set out in Law 18 930 to ensure a good compliance rate by these companies.

Bearer shares

172. A number of sanctions apply to both owners and issuing entities in the event of non-compliance with their reporting obligations; although no sanctions apply to the BCU, as a government authority.

Sanctions applied on non-compliant bearer share holders

173. Until 1 November 2014,, owners who failed to comply with their reporting obligations could not exercise their rights in relation to their equity interest, either as against the company or a third party, including rights to dividends (s. 8(a) of Law No. 18 930). Uruguay indicated that this suspension of rights also entailed that legal ownership could not be transferred by the non-compliant owner to another person, although this was not explicitly so stated in the law. Non-compliant owners were further subjected to administrative fines[27], ranging up to 100 times the amount set out in Article 95 of the Tax Code. The fines set out in Article 95 of the Tax Code range from UYU 240 to UYU 5.640 (USD 10 to USD 235) for 2014 (USD 1: UYU 24).

174. Since the entry into force of Law 19 288 on 1 November 2014, two mechanisms have been introduced. The first mechanism applies during the 90-day period following the entry into force of Law 19 288. Under Article 12 of Law 19 288, bearer share holders that do not fulfill their obligation to file an affidavit with the issuing entity within 90 days from the date of entry into force of Law 19 288 – until 29 January 2015 – will lose their capacity as shareholders. This loss of shareholder status entails the redemption of their respective shareholder's participation. From any payment made to the non-compliant bearer share holders in respect of the redemption of their participation, the company will have to deduct the fines payable under Article 8

27. Article 10 of Law 18 930.

of Law 18 930. The issuing entity shall require previously of the payment referred to in above paragraph, the certificate mentioned in the last paragraph of Article 6 of Law No. 18.930 or the certificate of direct registration with the Central Bank of Uruguay. Failure to comply with the above, will subject to a fine equivalent to 50% (fifty percent) of the amount which was unduly distributed to the non-compliant shareholder.

175. The second mechanism applies to any transfer of bearer shares. Under Art 16 (c) of Law 19 288, should a new bearer share holder fail to meet its reporting obligations within 90 days from the expiration of the term set out to report, he/she will lose his/her capacity as shareholder. From any payment made to the non-compliant bearer share holders equivalent to the redemption of his participation, the company will have to deduct the penalties payable under Article 8 of Law 18 930. Failure to comply with the above deduction will make the entity liable for the amount of the above sanction (Article 12 Law 19 288).

176. The amount of fines which may be applied, in addition to loss of shareholder status, depends upon the size of the issuing entity, the relative participation held by the shareholders in such entity and the length of time for which they have held the shares and ranges from UYU 5 000 to UYU 500 000 (approximately USD 250 to USD 25 000, ss. 8 of Law No. 18 930 and s. 17 of Decree No. 247/012). The National Internal Audit (AIN) is tasked with enforcement and collection of fines under this reporting regime (s. 4 of Law No. 18 930). 177. It was not clear under Law No 18 930 how fines could be collected from non-resident persons. Law 18 930 was applied such that the company could not make any distribution to the non-compliant non-resident shareholder. The Uruguayan authorities have confirmed that if a distribution is made, the company is fined with an amount equal to the dividends paid. In addition, the DGI suspends the clearance business certificate of the bearer share company. With Law 19 288, the participation of the non-compliant bearer share holder will have to be redeemed and the company will have to withhold the penalty on any distribution to the non-resident bearer share holders. This mechanism will ensure collection of penalties on the non-resident shareholders. As a practical matter, the AIN must collect the fines of the non-compliant bearer share holders (through the issuing entities which withhold the penalties). According to article 22 of Decree 346/014, the AIN will issue a guideline at the beginning of 2015, setting out the conditions under which the companies must communicate to the NIA the reduction of the equity capital pursuant to the loss of shareholder' status. Sanctions applied on non-compliant companies

177. Under Law 18 930, there are also significant sanctions on non-compliant entities. An entity which fails to report to the BCU "on time" may be presumed "inactive" and the General Taxation Office may discontinue

its certificate which is necessary for, amongst other things, the sale or levy of real estate, the distribution of profits or earnings and the initiation of proceedings in relation to commercial or industrial activities (s. 12 of Law No. 18 930 and art. 80 of Amended Text 1996, Title I).

178. In addition, relevant entities which do not comply with their reporting obligations cannot register any of their legal acts in the registers maintained by the General Registries Office (Art. 2 of Decree No. 24/013). Uruguayan authorities indicated that both these sanctions have a significant detrimental impact on the ability of such entities to conduct business or hold assets. Administrative fines also apply to entities for non-compliance: the level of fines for failure to report is the same as applicable to owners (s. 8 of Law No. 18 930 and s. 17 of the Supplementary Decree). Issuing entities which pay out dividends to a non-compliant owner are liable to a fine equal to the amount unduly distributed (s. 9 of Law No. 18 930). Representatives of the issuing entity are held personally liable for all penalties imposed upon the entity to the extent of his/her culpability (s. 9 of Law No. 18 930 and s. 17 of Decree No. 247/012). In practice, the AIN has launched 214 audits the scope of which includes, among others, checking whether the dividend distributions comply with Law 18 930. For this purpose, the AIN requested documentation: financial statements, minutes of shareholders meetings and book of attendance of shareholders meetings, and the Minutes of Board of Directors. To date, the AIN has analyzed the documentation provided in 55 cases.

179. As a general rule, bearer share companies must provide an affidavit representing 100% of the shareholders. Under Articles 1 and 4 of Law 19 288, a specific mechanism is put in place for companies that fail to provide an affidavit containing the ownership information representing more than 50% of the capital of the company within the 90-day period following the entry into force of Law 19 288. These failing companies shall be liquidated within 120 days from the expiration of the initial term of 90 days set forth in Article 1(1) of Law 19 288. The rationale of Law 19 288 is to clean-up all inactive companies at once, considering that it is presumed that all active companies will respond rather than being liquidated. Once the 120 day-term has expired, the company which have not been liquidated within 120 days will be subject to a fine representing 50% of its asset value (Article 4 of Law 19 288). The fine will be determined and collected by the AIN. In those cases, the penalties set out in articles 8 and 9 of Law 19.930, on the non-compliant companies and its non-compliant shareholders respectively, will not be applicable. The DGI will inform the NRC of the liquidation of the non-compliant companies. The NRC will publish a notice informing the public that the liquidation was carried out by operation of law. It is noted that in the case that a company provides 50% or more ownership information, Uruguay has mechanisms in place whereby the non-compliant bearer share holder will

be subject to enforcement measures (see section *Sanctions applied on non-compliant bearer share holders*).

180. Prior to Law 19 288, some concerns existed in relation to the exercise of these sanction powers in practice. In particular, a concern related to the ability of the BCU or the AIN to detect non-compliance with reporting obligations by the issuing entities in the context of the transfer of share ownership or change of shareholder information, as there was not a single uniform date for compliance by all relevant issuing entities (unlike the reporting obligations in relation to the initial transition period pursuant to s. 19 of Decree No. 247/012 where all such entities must report by 1 December 2012 in order to comply). However, it was noted in this regard that the AIN had powers to collect information deemed necessary from the BCU, issuing entities, owners and representatives for verification purposes and to ensure that the reporting obligations are complied with (s. 15 of Decree No. 247/012). Such checks could allow the AIN to detect the incidences of non-compliance with reporting obligations as described above. With the strengthening of the reporting obligations both on the companies and on the shareholders, the detection of non-compliance with reporting obligations by the issuing entities in the context of the transfer of share ownership or change of shareholder information will be made on an automatic basis. This detection will result from the obligation of the issuing entity to file an affidavit identifying 100% of the shareholders. In addition, founders or predecessors will be subject to penalties if their fail to ensure the registration of the new shareholders.

Monitoring process and sanctions

181. The BCU has implemented automated controls on the quality and consistency of affidavits entered into the registry. Missing documents, incorrect or incomplete data are rejected. This monitoring is carried out on a daily basis.

182. As a first step in the monitoring program, the AIN first cross-checked its database with those of the BCU and DGI via the following process:

1. The AIN first received the list of active bearer share companies from the DGI, together with information regarding their respective economic size and fiscal domicile. By May 8 2014, the total number of active bearer share companies amounted to 37 596. The AIN confirmed that information regarding the economic size of the bearer share companies is important because the determination of the penalty depends on the size of the entities. The fiscal domicile is important for inspection purposes.

2. As a second step, the AIN deducted from the total number of active bearer share companies those that complied with their identification requirements with the BCU. This represented 21 995 compliant bearer share companies on May 8, 2014.
3. Third, the AIN deducted from the total amount of active bearer share companies those which transformed their bearer share capital into nominative shares and were not recorded as such in the databases. The information was received from the NRC and represented 5 252 companies. Finally, from the BCU, they received a list of the infringing entities.

183. By May 8, 2014, 10 379 bearer share companies were infringing the provisions of Law 18 930. On May 22, 2014, the AIN informed the DGI of all the infringements. After a second cross-check and an update of the information, the AIN informed the DGI that 8 823 bearer share companies were non-compliant with the requirements of Law 18 930.

184. The DGI first suspended the clearance business certificate of those 8 823 bearer share companies, as set out in article 12 of Law 18 930, in stages. The suspension of the clearance certificate by the DGI can be a very effective sanction because the companies cannot carry out any activities in Uruguay without such certificate. For example, without a certificate, companies cannot issue and print invoices, participate in legal tenders, ask for any loans in the financial sector, or import or export or render services to the government. However, this sanction would not have any effect on foreign owned Uruguayan companies with no business operations in Uruguay.

Steps determining non-compliant bearer share companies (as of 22 May 2014)	
Active bearer share companies in the DGI database	37 596
Active bearer share companies compliant with the BCU requirements	– 21 965
Active bearer share companies which transformed their capital into nominative shares	-5 252
Non-compliant bearer share companies (first determination) by 8 May 2014	10 379
Active bearer share companies which transformed their capital into nominative shares between 8 May and 22 May 2014	-1 139
Active bearer share companies which complied with BCU requirements between 8 May and 22 May 2014	-367
Total non-compliant active bearer share companies on 22 May 2014	8 823

185. Out of those 8 823 bearer share companies, 2 487 bearer share companies came forward, either to denounce a mistake or to regularise their situations, such that only 6 336 active bearer share companies remained non-compliant. All the 6 336 infringing companies were notified of the infringement by registered telegram. When the AIN did not know the

address, the AIN published a note in the official gazette. Out of the 6 336, 428 acknowledged the penalty and 370 presented objections. Out of the 370, 30% were encouraged to comply. As of 21 July 2014, 315 corporations were issued penalties pursuant to Article 4(c) of the law 18930, the rest is being processed. The minimum fine imposed is USD 10 000 and maximum is USD 30 000. The non-compliant companies had their "clearance business certificate" suspended, which means they cannot carry out business in Uruguay nor pay out dividends. The DGI also suspends clearance certificates of bearer share companies that do not comply with their obligation to file a tax return. The compliance rate of bearer share corporations (60% in 2012) has been lower than that of nominative share corporations (85% in 2012). To address the filing deficit of bearer share companies identified in 2012 and 2013, the DGI suspended 15 009 clearance certificates in 2014.

186. Additionally, the AIN established guidelines for the situations where the bearer shareholders voluntarily pay the fines (for example when there is a transfer, and the buyer is liable for the fine). Additional assurance has been introduced in guidelines, for example in situations where the shares become nominative shares, the company has to state that it has no pending penalties. This statement is required at the NRC when the amendment is registered. Partnerships.

187. The sale or assignment of stakeholdings in business partnerships (which include both SRLs and partnerships), apart from those in corporations or partnerships limited by shares must be registered with the DGI within 30 days, prior to registration with the General Registries Office (s. 22 of Law No. 18 930; s. 1 of Decree No. 242/012). The Uruguayan authorities indicated that this requirement sets out an obligation within the remit of the DGI; therefore Section 95 of the Tax Code applies in the event of non-compliance. Under Section 95 of the Tax Code, violation of laws or regulations passed by "the corresponding bodies that determine formal duties" is punishable by a fine ranging from UYU 240 to UYU 5.640 (USD 10 to USD 235) for 2014 (USD 1: UYU 24). Between August 1st, 2012 and May 31st, 2014, the DGI registered 1 635 sales or assignments of stockholdings in SRL and business partnerships. The tax filing compliance rate of SRL and partnerships ranges from 72% to 75% in 2012 and 2013. As a general rule, the DGI suspended the clearance business certificate of the non-compliant SRL and partnerships, with the effect that they cannot carry on business in Uruguay and cannot pay out dividends, until they file their tax return and get their clearance certificate back.

Trusts

188. Professional trustees who fail to comply with the registration and information obligations by the Trusts Law are subject to the same sanctions

imposed on financial intermediaries (article 12, Trusts Law). During the period under review, the BCU has not applied sanctions on professional trustees for breaches of their registration and information obligations.

Foundations

189. Under s27 of the Foundation Law, the Civil Association Agency has the power to demand all necessary information to ensure that the foundation is in compliance with the Foundations Law. In the event of non-compliance, sanctions may be imposed by the Agency, including fines.

Conclusion of enforcement measures

190. A combination of enforcement measures are in force in Uruguay to ensure the availability of ownership and identity information in respect of companies, partnerships and trusts by the DGI, the NRC and the AIN. In the two income tax cases answered by Uruguay, ownership information has been made available in a timely manner in one case relating to bearer shares.

191. In regards to bearer shares, Uruguay has devoted significant resources to ensure the monitoring of the 2012 Laws and has addressed the deficiencies identified in the Phase 1 supplementary report. Further, Uruguay has actively imposed sanctions in cases of non-compliance with the requirements of Law 18 930. In addition, Uruguay has addressed the deficiencies it identified in practice in respect of inactive bearer share companies, which it discovered during the implementation of Law 18 930, by enacting Law 19 288 and Decree 346/014. Nevertheless, as Law 19 288 is recent, it has not been tested in practice. Uruguay should continue to monitor that information on the owners of bearer shares is made fully available in all cases.

192. In light of the above, it was concluded that the phase 1 aspect of Element A.1 be upgraded from "in place but in need of improvement" to "in place". The overall Phase 2 rating is determined to be Largely Compliant.

Determination and factors underlying recommendations

Determination
The element is in place.

Phase 2 Rating	
Largely compliant	
Factors underlying recommendations	**Recommendations**
Legal requirements have been introduced for the reporting of ownership information in relation to bearer shares in all cases. However, some of these legal requirements such as the extinction of shareholder rights for non-reporting and the mandatory liquidation of non-compliant bearer share companies, have only recently come into force and their effectiveness could not be assessed in practice by the assessment team.	Uruguay should continue to monitor the mandatory liquidation of non-compliant bearer share companies and ensure that information on the owners of bearer shares is made fully available in all cases.

A.2. Accounting records

Jurisdictions should ensure that reliable accounting records are kept for all relevant entities and arrangements.

General requirements (ToR A.2.1)

Commerce Code

193. Chapter III of the Commercial Code sets out the requirements on every "trader" in respect of accounting records. The definition of "trader" is provided by article 1 of the Commercial Code:

> "A person who acting in his legal capacity who trades for his own benefit, making it a habitual occupation and who is registered in the NRC."

194. This definition encompasses all "business partnerships" formed under the provisions of the Business Partnerships Law.

195. Traders must keep a journal, inventory book and letter copy book (section 55, Commercial Code). The precise requirements for each book are set out in Title II, Chapter III, of the Commercial Code, relevantly:

> **Section 56.** In the Journal there will be registered day by day, chronologically all the operations performed by the trader, either bills of exchange or any other credit bills he might give, of his own or of someone else, by virtue of any title, so that each entry

> shows who is the creditor and who is the debtor in the corresponding operation.
>
> As to the entries corresponding to domestic expenses, these can be registered globally, with the date they went out of petty cash. …
>
> **Section 59**. The inventory book shall be opened with the exact description of the money, chattels, real property, credits, and any other kind of valuables making up the trader's capital at the time he begins his course of business.
>
> Afterwards, and during the first three months of each year, every trader shall register in that same book, the balance sheet of his course of business, including in it all his properties, credits and shares, as well as all his outstanding debts and obligations at the date of the balance sheet, with no reserve or omission whatsoever.
>
> Inventories and balance sheets shall be signed by all those who have a stake in the business, and who are present at the time of its constitution. …
>
> **Section 61.** In the companies' inventories and balance sheets it shall be enough to state the common property and obligations of the association, without including the private ones of each associate. …
>
> **Section 63.** In the letter copybook, traders shall copy entirely the text of all the letters written relating to their business.
>
> They are likewise obliged to keep in files and in good order all the letters they receive regarding their negotiations, writing down overleaf the date on which they answered them, or specifying, in the same way, that they did not answer them.

196. All three books (journal, inventory book, letter copybook) must be authorised and sealed by a Civil Court (Article 65 Commercial Code) and submitted to the NRC for approval on an annual basis (article 51, NRC Law).

197. These requirements are sufficient to correctly explain all transactions, the financial position of the trader, and to allow financial statements to be prepared. All traders must keep their books for 20 years from the termination of the business or trade (article 80). The Commerce Code does not however specify any express requirements to retain underlying documentation. Traders will also be subject to the tax law obligations described below, to the extent of their taxable operations, and, pursuant to a 2012 decree, even those entities not subject to tax are now subject to obligations to maintain underlying documentation.

198. Uruguay has advised that the Commercial Code is intended to regulate matters of private law. Therefore, sanctions for failure to keep the required accounting records relate to presumptions to be made against the relevant person in the event of a dispute. For instance, accounting records that do not meet the requirements of the Code "are of no value in any legal proceeding to benefit the person whose records are being examined" (article 67, Commercial Code) (see section A.1.6 above on Enforcement measures concerning domestic companies).

Business Partnerships Law

199. In addition to the Commercial Code requirements which are imposed on all traders, the Business Partnerships Law which governs all "business partnerships" (which includes companies and partnerships) also imposes some accounting record requirements. The obligations under this law are intended to facilitate the control of partners and shareholders over the management of the entity by administrators. The Business Partnerships Law (article 87 ff) sets out accounting record obligations which includes the maintenance of an inventory of assets and debts, balance sheet and a profit proposal if is applicable. The Business Partnerships Law does not however specify any express requirements to retain underlying documentation. Business partnerships will also be subject to the tax law obligations described below to the extent of their taxable operations.

200. For SAs, article 332 and following of the Business Partnerships Law also requires the maintenance of accounting books, in addition to the mandatory books required for every trader. Article 1 of Decree 266/007 provides that corporations must keep such accounting books in accordance with the International Financial Reporting Standards adopted by the Council of International Accounting Standards (International Accounting Standards Board-IASB). Compliance with these ensures that the accounting books are comprehensive and allow the preparation of financial statements. At minimum, the accounting books must include a balance sheet; statement; statement of origin and application of funds; statement of changes in equity, and notes to financial statements.

201. As a general rule, business partnerships with total assets exceeding USD 950 000 or annual revenue greater than USD 3 million are required to register their financial statements which comply with IFRS with the AIN. Failure to register financial statements means that that the business partnership may not distribute profits and is liable to a fine of up to USD 270 000 (article 97bis, Business Partnerships Law). In addition, pursuant to article 24 of Law 18 930 (Registration of financial statements), a specific filing obligation applies to companies, associations and agricultural partnerships, trusts and investment funds not supervised by the BCU, which derive income that

is not taxable in Uruguay. Such entities, deriving more than UI 4 million (approx. USD 500 000), must register their financial statements with the AIN under the same conditions and requirements set out article 97 Bis of the Business Partnership Act (see paragraph 215).

Trusts

202. In respect of trusts created under Uruguayan law, all trustees (general and professional) are required to (Article 19, Law No. 17 703 of 4 November 2003 (the "Trusts Law")):

> a) keep an inventory and a separate accounting of the assets, rights and debts that form the trust property… in all cases, the accounting shall be based on proper rules".

203. Prior to 2012, the Tax Code set out requirements for the keeping of reliable accounting records and underlying documentation for a minimum of five years which applied to all trusts except for guarantee trusts. The Trusts Law itself did not set out any requirements for the maintenance of reliable accounting records and underlying documents for any minimum period of time. Therefore, to the extent that a trust was not subject to tax in Uruguay or was not a "taxpayer"(i.e. in the case of guarantee trusts), it was not subject to requirements to keep reliable accounting records and underlying documentation for any minimum period of time. However, the accounting record requirements for financial intermediaries and under the AML regime were also applicable where the trust was managed by a professional (including financial) trustee.

204. Trusts created under Uruguayan law (and the trustee as the "tax responsible" for the trust), and since 2012 trusts that are not subject to tax, will however be subject to the record-keeping obligations established by tax law (as described below).

205. Further record retention requirements are set out in relation to trusts which are not subject to tax in Uruguay. Trusts which are subject to BCU supervision, which includes all trusts (including guarantee trusts) managed by professional trustees, are subject to requirements to maintain reliable accounting records and underlying documentation for a minimum period of ten years (Section 255 of the compilation of BCU regulations, updated to 28 June 2012). Failure to comply with the record keeping requirements under the BCU regulations is punishable by the service of a subpoena, fines and/or suspension or termination of the person's activities on the securities market (Section 286 of the BCU regulations).

206. Trusts which are not subject to BCU supervision (i.e. those mentioned by general trustees) are subject to requirement under section 23 of Law No. 18 930 to maintain underlying documentation for a period of ten years.

Foundations

207. Foundations must only be created for not for profit purposes under Uruguayan law and are closely regulated by the Ministry of Culture and Education. They are subject to obligations to keep accounting records under article 25 of the Foundations Law which provides that accounting records should be based on reports as set out in the regulations; however such regulations have not been evaluated.

Tax rules

208. Tax Code obligations are applicable to all tax payers who must determine their taxable basis. A definition of taxpayers was inserted by article 9 of the Tax Reform Law 18 083 (Tax Reform Law), and includes:

(a) business partnerships (including Free Trade Zone companies), with or without legal status, residing in Uruguay, even those undergoing liquidation;

(b) permanent establishment of entities not residing in Uruguay; …

(c) Closed credit investment funds;

(d) trusts except for guarantee trusts;

(e) individuals and condominiums, whenever they receive any covered income;

(f) associations and foundations in respect of their taxable operations mentioned in article 5, Title III herein.

209. Taxpayers must determine their taxable income according to rules described in Decree Law 150/2007 (the Company Tax Law) as modified by Decree Law 208/2007. These rules include requirements relating to the determination of costs, expenditures, adjustments, and asset valuation amongst other matters. According to the Company Tax Law, taxpayers must generally determine their taxable income based on "adequate accounting" records.

210. The Tax Code requires the taxpayer, and "responsible persons" (for example trustees in respect of trusts) to keep records relating to their "taxable operations". Article 70 of the Tax Code provides that they must:

- keep the books and the special registers, and document the taxable operations according to the provisions set forth by law, regulations or the resolutions of tax-collecting institutions;

- maintain orderly accounting records and other documents and records until the expiry of the statute of limitation for imposing tax liabilities;
- submit or exhibit before the fiscal offices or before the authorised officials the returns, reports, vouchers of the legitimate source of goods, and any other documentation related to facts that might generate tax obligations, and provide them with the addenda or explanations they might request.

211. In addition, filing requirements set out Article 24 of Law 18 930 for those entities that are not subject to a tax filing obligation are further implemented by Decree No. 242/012 dated 1 August 2012 amending section 56 of Decree No. 597/988. Under Section 2 of Decree No 242/012 the requirement to keep books, documents and correspondence at one's place of domicile, which originally only applied to taxpayers, also applies to "[b]usiness corporations, associations and agricultural partnerships, trusts, investment funds, civil societies and foundations" that are not subject to tax in Uruguay. Uruguayan authorities indicate that "books, documents and correspondence" includes "mandatory accounting books". Uruguay indicated that a breach of Section 56 of Decree No. 597/988 (as amended) is a breach of a tax standard and financial penalties, ranging from UYU 240 to UYU 5 640 (USD 10 to USD 235) for 2014, would apply pursuant to section 95 of the Tax Code.

Financial intermediaries

212. All persons carrying out "financial intermediation" activities are regulated in Uruguay by the BCU pursuant to Decree Law 15 322. Article 14 of that Law authorises the BCU to regulate the record keeping requirements and the information they should send to BCU. Book V of the BCU regulation refers to the comprehensive transaction (and client identity) records that must be kept by financial intermeediaries (being persons subject to the supervision of the BCU) and these are described in Section A.1.3.

Anti-money laundering regime

213. Regulation under the AML regime covers a broad class of persons including financial intermediaries and the BCU has issued specific regulations relating to record-keeping in respect of money exchange institutions, credit management companies, securities exchange users, investment fund managers, and money transfer companies amongst others. Those requirements depend on the structure of each particular institution; however in all cases the information required to be kept is limited to that which is relevant to suspicious transaction reports.

Underlying documentation (ToR A.2.2)

214. To the extent that a taxpayer undertakes taxable operations, the Tax Code requires that all relevant accounting information, including underlying documents, be kept for a minimum period of 5 years. Until 2012, there was some doubt regarding those relevant taxpayers that did not undertake "taxable operations", for example, those operating in the Free Trade Zone or those persons with only non-Uruguayan source income. Uruguayan authorities considered that regardless of the source or nature of income (as taxable or not), documentation had to be maintained in order to prove that in fact the income was not taxable. In order to avoid any doubt in this regard it was recommended that Uruguay include a specific requirement for all relevant entities and arrangements, regardless of their tax liability, to maintain underlying documentation for at least 5 years.

215. Section 56 of Decree No. 597/988 (as amended by Section 2 of Decree No. 242/012) provides an obligation for the keeping of underlying records for entities not subject to tax in Uruguay, which addresses the above-mentioned concern in relation to the maintenance of underlying documentation by relevant companies and partnerships not subject to Uruguay tax. However, as these provisions introduce new obligations on entities not previously subject to the control of the DGI, it is recommended that Uruguay's enforcement and monitoring powers are sufficiently exercised in practice to ensure the availability of underlying accounting documentation in these cases.

216. Where a transaction is carried out by a financial intermediary, all underlying documentation will also be kept. Book V of the BCU Regulations requires all financial intermediaries (being all entities subject to supervision by the BCU) are required to keep all client identity and transaction information Further, in some cases, this information will be required to be sent to the BCU, for example in the case of unusual transactions or those above particular monetary thresholds. These requirements imposed on financial intermediaries are described further in section A.3 below.

217. In addition, under the AML regime, where financial transactions exceed certain thresholds financial intermediaries must keep all records and business correspondence necessary to reconstruct those financial transactions (article 73, Decree Law 14 294, as modified by Law 17 016).

218. In practice, Uruguay has provided underlying documentation in responses to an EOI request for accounting information made during the review period. The Uruguayan authorities have indicated that they provided underlying documentation in the form of invoices and contracts and that they did not have any difficulty obtaining this information.

Document retention (ToR A.2.3)

219. According to the Commercial Code all traders must keep their books for 20 years from the termination of the business or trade (article 80, Commercial Code and article 307.4 BCU Regulation). The Tax Code requires that records be maintained for a minimum of 5 years (articles 38 and 70 C) Tax Code). The main consequence relies on the DGI's power to make an imputed determination of taxes where records are insufficient (article 66 Tax Code). In certain cases the failure to keep accounting books and underlying documentation will, with other circumstances, permit a presumption of the intention to commit fraud (article 96, Tax Code). The BCU Regulations (article 307.4) requires the financial intermediary to keep all relevant records which may be required by the BCU for a minimum period of 10 years. In case of non compliance, penalties range from a written admonition to the revocation of the authorisation to operate, and in serious cases where fraud is established, criminal sanctions may be applied. The number of audits carried out by the DGI are set out in paragraph 226.

220. Section 56 of Decree No. 597/988 (as amended by Section 2 of Decree No. 242/012) provides for a minimum 5 year-holding period in relation to the keeping of accounting records and underlying documentation by trusts not subject to tax.

Monitoring and enforcement activities carried out by the AIN and the DGI

221. As mentioned in paragraph 205, the filing requirements with the AIN apply to *(i)* any entity with total assets exceeding USD 950 000 or annual revenue greater than USD 3 million and *(ii)* to companies, associations and agricultural partnerships, trusts and investment funds not supervised by the BCU, which are not subject to tax in Uruguay, and derive income in excess of UI 4 000 000 (approx. USD 500 000). Pursuant to article 313 of Law 18 996, which entered into force on 1 January 2013, in the case that a company does not register its financial records with the AIN, the clearance business certificate, which is necessary to carry on business in Uruguay, may be suspended. The total or partial breach of the obligation to exhibit books and accounting records constitutes one of the presumptions for the determination of taxes on an assumed basis (Article 66 Tax Code) and one of the presumptions of the subjective element of administrative offense (Fraud: Paragraph e) Article 96 Tax Code). The Uruguayan authorities have confirmed that no clearance certificates have been suspended by the AIN during the peer review period, as article 313 of Law 18 996 only entered into force on 1 January 2013. As the Article 24 filing requirements are quite recent, Uruguay is recommended to ensure that its monitoring and enforcement powers are sufficiently exercised in practice to reinforce the legal requirements which ensure the availability of

accounting information in all cases. In 2014, the AIN worked on implementing e-filing of financial records, as part of a project to improve information transparency of markets through the existence of a sustained and effective process of adoption of international financial reporting standards.

222. Regarding the monitoring activities carried out by the DGI, the Large Taxpayer Division has carried out 42 tax audits in 2011 and 2012, respectively and 45 tax audits in 2013; whereas the Control Division in charge of the other taxpayers has carried out 1 336 tax audits in 2011, 1 381 tax audits in 2012 and 1 294 tax audits in 2013. During these audits, the tax administration checks amongst other items, the availability and the quality of accounting records and underlying documents. The penalties that are applied are not in general specific to the availability of accounting records, but take into account the whole assessment of the tax audit carried out.

223. For domestic purposes, concerning the determination of taxes on an assumed basis arising from the total or partial breach of the obligation to exhibit accounting records during the period under review, the TCA (*Tribunal en lo Contencioso Administrativo*) Administrative Law Court rendered 14 sentences during the peer review period. In six cases, the Tribunal did not accept the determination of taxes on an assumed basis, whereas in six other cases it upheld the resolution. In the last two cases, the Tribunal accepted the determination only partially. A total of 11 cases for determination of taxes on an assumed basis are being processed (no sentence has been passed) due to total or partial breach of the obligation to exhibit accounting records. As for the charges of tax fraud (specifically related to Paragraph e) Article 96) over the period under review, the Administrative Appeals Tribunal rendered 3 sentences: two of which did not accept the charges of tax fraud and one which confirmed the charge of tax fraud. A total of 3 tax fraud cases are currently being processed.

Availability of accounting information in practice

224. The Uruguayan authorities have confirmed that, during the three-year period under review, there were 19 requests for accounting information relating to Uruguayan entities, but 12 of them concerned VAT requests and therefore fall out of the scope of this review. Accounting information was provided in three cases regarding companies out of seven income tax cases. The non-provision of accounting information in four cases pertained to matters regarding the interpretation of the entry into force provision of one EOI agreement (see section C.1.9 *Be given effect through domestic law*), and not to availability of accounting information.

225. The information requested included information on accounting records, invoices and financial statements. In the case considered valid by

Uruguay, the information was available and provided in a timely manner. In one case, this information was retrieved directly from the taxpayer. Feedback from peers who received the information confirms that no issue has arisen with obtaining accounting information.

Determination and factors underlying recommendations

Determination
The element is in place.

Phase 2 Rating	
Largely Compliant	
Experience of monitoring the record keeping requirements in respect of underlying accounting documentation and the filing requirements of annual accounts, which apply to entities not subject to tax since August 2012, is limited.	Uruguay should ensure that its monitoring and enforcement powers are sufficiently exercised in practice to support the record keeping and filing requirements applicable to entities not subject to tax in Uruguay

A.3. Banking information

Banking information should be available for all account-holders.

Record-keeping requirements (ToR A.3.1)

Anti-money laundering regime

226. Banks, as well as all other persons carrying out "financial intermediation" activities are regulated in Uruguay by the BCU (Law Decree 15 322), which is a key component of Uruguay's anti-money laundering regime. Financial intermediation is defined as (article 1):

> the habitual and professional trading operations or mediation between supply and demand for securities, cash and precious metals.

227. The BCU is authorised to regulate the record keeping requirements and the information that financial intermediaries should send to BCU (article 14, Decree Law 15 322). According to Circular 1 978/2008, financial intermediaries cannot maintain accounts or manage transactions for clients whom they have not properly identified. This requirement is applicable not only for habitual clients but also to clients who perform one-off or occasional transactions.

228. To meet those client identity requierments, financial intermediaries must obtain identity information in order to be able to verify it and record it, as well as information in respect of the purpose and nature of the business relationship. The precise nature of the identity information requested and the verification procedures will depend on the type of account or transaction involved, the amount volume of funds and the risk assessment carried out by the financial intermediary.

229. Circular 1 978/2008 states that financial intermediaries should define systematic procedures for identifying new customers, and not establish a "definite" commercial relationship until it has successfully verified their identity. In addition, they must establish procedures that allow regular updating of information on existing customers, especially in the case of higher risk customers. In addition, there are also provisions to identify the ultimate controler of the accounts, and to establish "reasonable measures" in order to know the clients property structure and control.

230. The Circular provides that the minimum client identity information that financial intemediaries should require is:

- For individuals: completed name, place and date of birth, identity documentation, marital status (incuding spouse information), address and phone number, occupation, and income. It must be stated whether the client is acting on behalf of someone else, abd in which case that other person should be identified. The same information should be obtained in respect of agents or representatives of the client.
- For legal entities: name, incorporation date, address and phone number, taxpayer registration number, and other documentation, such as an authorised copy of the entity's incorporation contract, registration in the NRC and documents proving the power of agents or representative to act on their behalf. Other information to be collected should include the entity's main activity, average income, and ownership structure, including its ultimate controlling entity. Provision of the ownership structure should include persons holding 10% or mores of shares.

231. In respect of occasional clients who in one calendar year do not perform transactions which total more than USD 30 000 or its equivalent in other currency, financial intermediaries should require them to provide: their full name, identity documentation, address and phone number in case of individuals; and in the case of legal entities, their name, address, phone number, tax registration number (if applicable) and identification of the individual who is acting on the entity's behalf.

232. Book V of the BCU Regulation sets out information requirements and penalties. Pursuant to article 305, the BCU has the right to ask any financial intermediary to produce any documents relating to their clients and

the transactions carried out for those clients. Further, article 307.1 specifies that a financial intermediary must keep all documents which the BCU may ask you to produce, and they must be retained for a minimum 10 year period (article 307.4). In addition to these comprehensive requirements, for certain transactions which for example are unusual or above a certain monetary threshold, financial intermediaries must communicate all information relating to the transaction to the BCU (article 374.1).

Monitoring of the banks in practice

233. The supervision of the financial sector in Uruguay is carried out by the BCU. The BCU was created in 1967 and employs 700 staff members. A department of 200 staff members headed by a superintendent supervises all financial institutions in Uruguay. This includes the banks, the insurance market, the currency exchange and the brokers. The supervision can be desk based or in the form of onsite inspections. Annual planning is based on risk assessment. Uruguay is a member of GAFILATI and the Egmont Group in Brussels. The last evaluation was carried out in 2009. Under the know-your-client (KYC) rules and the rules regarding the origin of the funds, the financial entities must keep the information regarding the transactions and their clients for a period of 10 years. They also must report suspicious activities.

234. The financial institutions include 14 commercial banks (2 state-owned and 12 private, foreign-owned banks), 1 co-operative financial institution, 5 finance houses ("casas financieras"), 3 offshore financial institutions ("instituciones financieras externas" or "IFEs"), and 4 pension funds managing companies.

235. The BCU is also involved in the supervision with respect to compliance with obligations under the AML regime. Ten employees are allocated to financial intelligence and 11 employees deal with supervision. There are 20 financial intermediaries, 90 securities market brokers, 90 currency exchanges brokers, and 20 insurance companies in Uruguay which are subject to the supervision of the BCU.

236. The monitoring carried out by the BCU consists in desktop morni-toring and onsite visits. Under the desktop monitoring procedure, external auditors of banks, securities market brokers, insurance brokers, and currency exchange brokers have to provide samples of various files, which are checked by the BCU staff members. Onsite inspections are carried out following a set procedure. The inspector uses a standard questionnaire, checks the compliance with KYC procedures and checks a sample of files. At the end of the inspection, a report is sent to the institution. A follow-up plan is requested from the institution to address the recommendations made. In addition, if

serious or recurrent non-compliance is observed, penalties are applied. Banks are usually inspected once every two years. Depending on the size of the entity, the onsite visit lasts between 15 and 30 days. For smaller institutions, the onsite visit last between 10 and 15 days. Throughout the course of the onsite inspection program, compliance with AML obligations has been found to be satisfactory.

237. The BCU conducted 16 on-site supervision activities of financial institutions in 2011, 12 in 2012 and 11 in 2013. As a result of its periodical on-site visits, the Superintendence drafts a final report containing an assessment of each entity's economic and financial situation, solvency and liquidity, corporate governance, compliance with due diligence requirements and the way it manages the main risks faced in the activity developed. Different weaknesses that have been identified include, e.g. in internal risk management issues, and other basic management standards to be met by entities. These are summarised in a closing note, in which the supervisor lists the weaknesses detected and their importance (deserving priority attention or other weaknesses) giving the entity a term so that the entity may respond formulating an action plan to solve the weaknesses. During the period between August, 2012 and April 2014, nine fines were imposed on financial entities which did not comply with the AML/CFT legislation. The lowest fine imposed amounted to USD 19 541, whereas the highest fine amounted to USD 81 768. The listings of all the sanctions applied to both financial intermediation entities and other types of financial entities by the SSF are published monthly in the BCU's webpage, and can therefore be accessed by the general public.

238. When serious breaches are detected, or when the entity supervised fails to show the necessary degree of commitment and has not made its best efforts to fulfill the action plan formulated, the application of a sanction to the entity is considered, which can range from an warning to a fine, and in more serious cases, more serious measures can be adopted such as the intervention or the cancellation of the license to operate. During the peer review period, the BCU revoked four bank licenses.

239. Additionally, other sanctions are applicable in the following cases:

- Errors or delays in submitting the information to the Superintendence by financial entities. The BCU applied 536 sanctions (split between: 15 observation; seven warning and 514 fines) during the peer review period. The highest fine amounted to USD 27 400;
- Non-compliance with technical ratios (risk limitation, guarantees, etc.). The BCU applied 48 fines, the highest of which amounted to USD 374 173; and

- Non-compliance with other standards (CDD obligations). The BCU applied 8 fines during the peer review period. The highest fine amounted to 38 728.

Availability of banking information in practice

240. During the peer review period, Uruguay received ten requests covering banking information. Eight of the requests concerned companies and two concerned individuals. Banking information was exchanged in five cases (see also section B.1.5 below on *Access to Bank Information*). All of these requests were made after 2 January 2011, and concerned periods after 2 January 2011.

241. Over the review period, banking information was generally available in Uruguay and was accessed directly from the taxpayers (see section B.1.5 on *Access to Bank Information* and section B.2. *Notification Requirements and Rights and Safeguards*). The non-provision of banking information in five cases pertained to the interpretation of the entry into force provision of one EOI agreement (see section C.1.9 *Be given effect through domestic law*), and not to availability of banking information.

Conclusion

242. Overall, the legal and regulatory framework in Uruguay provides for the availability of banking information. In addition to anti-money laundering requirements, banking is a regulated industry, subject to ongoing surveillance and monitoring by the BCU, to ensure compliance with licensing regulations and record keeping requirements. The BCU has a large array of sanctions at its disposal, permitting it to appropriately tailor the fine to the level of breach. Ultimately, a bank can lose its licence. Therefore, sanctions appear to be fixed at an appropriate level to be dissuasive enough to deter non-compliance. Moreover, penalties are actively enforced in practice where entities are found to be in breach of their information keeping requirements.

243. Over the three-year period under review, Uruguay received ten EOI requests concerning banking information, of which information was retrieved by the Uruguayan authorities directly from the taxpayer in five cases. The banking information requested included account statements, signatory authorisation, instructions given by account holder to the bank for the operation of the accounts, paying-in and disbursement slips, written remittance orders, detailed records of deposits and withdrawals, and wire transfers. Feedback from peers has not indicated any issues with the availability of banking information.

Determination and factors underlying recommendations

Phase 1 Determination
The element is in place.

Phase 2 Rating
Compliant

B. Access to Information

Overview

244. A variety of information may be needed in a tax enquiry and jurisdictions should have the authority to obtain all such information. This includes information held by banks and other financial institutions as well as information concerning the ownership of companies or the identity of interest holders in other persons or entities, such as partnerships and trusts, as well as accounting information in respect of all such entities. This section of the report examines whether Uruguay's legal and regulatory framework gives the authorities access powers that cover the right types of persons and information and whether rights and safeguards would be compatible with effective exchange of information.

245. Uruguay's ability to obtain information for exchange of information (EOI) purposes is based on the broad powers granted to the DGI which are found in its Tax Code. Generally, those powers provide for access to all types of information, notwithstanding from whom such information was obtained. A special court-based regime is in place for accessing information otherwise subject to bank secrecy. While legislation was amended to expressly provide for the lifting of banking secrecy for the purposes of an EOI request, such provision only applied to bank information from 2 January 2011 and not to information prior to that date which might nevertheless be relevant to an EOI request. In addition, prior to 2012, for information held by trustees, in some cases where access was sought to information where the trust was not subject to tax in Uruguay, a duty of confidentiality could impede access. Uruguay has adequately addressed this issue through introduction of an express override to trustee confidentiality in Law No. 18 930. However, there has been no new development in Uruguay in respect of access to banking information prior to 2 January 2011, such that the Phase 1 determination for element B.1 remains "in place but certain aspects of its legal implementation need improvement".

246. In practice, access powers are rarely used to gather identity and ownership information as most of the time the information is available with the tax authorities. Accounting and banking information have been accessed directly from the taxpayer. When necessary, the gathering of ownership and accounting information for EOI purposes is performed with exactly the same measures as the gathering of information for domestic tax purposes, and has been effective for accessing information in those cases.

247. In respect of the rights and safeguards allowed to persons concerned by an EOI request, Uruguay's law generally ensures that there are no impediments to effective access to relevant information. Prior to 2011, the judicial process for accessing bank information lacked any exceptions to the obligation of prior notification which meant that effective access and exchange of information may be impeded. Uruguay has brought into force Decree No. 313/011 which sets out procedures in relation to exchange of information by Uruguay, under its DTCs and TIEAs. Amongst other things, Decree No. 313/011, as modified by Decree No. 378/013 contains a prior notification provision, under which all persons who are the subject of the requested information and who are tax residents in Uruguay must be notified, without any clear exception. This notification requirement takes place after the information has been gathered and is merely a notification for the taxpayer to see the information that will be sent to the requesting jurisdiction, without naming the requesting jurisdiction. This opportunity is only available for five days, and does not constitute a suspensive measure. In addition, the person with access to the information is not entitled to any appeal or judicial proceeding. Even if no person who received such a notification has consulted its file in the premises of the DGI during the peer review period, the absence of exception to prior notification may potentially hinder effective exchange of information. Accordingly, the recommendation made in the Phase 1 supplementary report that the application of appropriate exceptions should be clarified to ensure that the notification requirement does not hinder effective exchange of information, has not been removed even if the gap appears limited in practice.

248. The named competent authority under EOI agreements (both DTCs and TIEAs) is the Minister of the Economy and Finance. This power is delegated by resolution to the head of the DGI who has delegated this authority internally within the DGI to the deputy director of the DGI, the head of the large taxpayer unit and the head of the International Tax Department (ITD).

249. Uruguay received 17 income tax requests for information over the review period including requests for ownership, banking and accounting information. Each request could cover more than one type of requested information. Not all the requested information (ownership, accounting and banking information) in each request was gathered from the same source. In those 5 cases where information was provided or partially provided,

the information was accessed from the databases available to the DGI in 4 cases, and from third parties (such as the taxpayer or another holder of the information in 4 cases. When accessed from a third party a letter setting out the requested information is drafted and hand delivered and this is usually expected to be provided at the time of delivery. In some cases third parties were issued a summons to appear at the offices of the DGI in person to deliver the information. In no cases did the taxpayer or a third party refuse to provide the information and search warrants or the use of compulsory powers were not necessary to be applied over the review period for the purposes of EOI.

B.1. Competent Authority's ability to obtain and provide information

Competent authorities should have the power to obtain and provide information that is the subject of a request under an exchange of information arrangement from any person within their territorial jurisdiction who is in possession or control of such information (irrespective of any legal obligation on such person to maintain the secrecy of the information).

Ownership and identity information (ToR B.1.1) and Accounting records (ToR B.1.2)

250. Under Uruguayan law, the DGI has general access powers, and there is also a specific regime to access information held by financial intermediaries which would otherwise be subject to bank secrecy (see Section B.1.5).

251. The DGI has full powers of investigation and inspection to carry out all steps necessary for the achievement of "tax purposes". Uruguay has advised that tax purposes should be interpreted broadly and includes when the information is requested to comply with information exchange requests. Article 68 of the Tax Code sets out a non-exhaustive list of possible measures that could be taken by the DGI:

- inspect or take possession of books, documents held by taxpayers and other responsible persons [that is, persons who under the tax law have a legal responsibility for the taxpayer's tax obligations. For example trustees in respect of trusts], and require such to appear before the DGI to provide information (article 68A).
- carry out inspections of personal or real property held by taxpayers. Private residences may only be searched after a warrant has been obtained (article 68C).
- require information from third parties when it considers it necessary (article 68E).

252. In addition, article 70 of the Tax Code sets-out a mandatory obligation to provide the requested information in tax matters.

253. Uruguay has advised that it is not necessary for a notice to be issued to the person concerned in order to exercise the powers under article 68. Likewise, it is not necessary to commence an audit in order to exercise those powers. The exercise of all administrative powers must however be recorded in writing, in detailed records signed by the relevant officials, with a copy furnished to interested parties upon request (articles 44 and 45, Tax Code).

254. The DGI's powers to access information are broad, and generally allow it to obtain all relevant information regardless of its type (for example, ownership, accounting or bank information) or from whom it is to be obtained (for example, taxpayers or third parties). However, in some cases, a few possible impediments to accessing information which may not be consistent with the standard are identified below, in respect of access to bank information.

Preliminary assessment of the validity of incoming requests

255. Section 5 of Decree No. 313/011, as amended by Decree No. 253/012 of 8 August 2012, provides that in performing its preliminary assessment of the validity of an incoming EOI request, the DGI must ensure that the request includes, as a minimum:

- elements allowing for it to identify the people or entities to which the requested information corresponds;
- elements allowing for it to identify people or entities who have, control or possess, within Uruguay's borders, the requested information;
- the period of time to which the information requested relates;
- detail of the requested information; and
- the tax purpose for which the information is requested.

256. Uruguay advised that the identification elements required under this provision are interpreted consistently with those provided in Article 5(5) of the Model TIEA, in particular, the wording "elements allowing for it to identify the peoples or entities to which the requested information corresponds" is to be interpreted in line with Article 5(5)(e) of the Model TIEA. Section 5 of Decree No. 313/011 is meant to ensure that the requesting state demonstrates the foreseeable relevance of a request. The Uruguayan authorities indicated that they will inform their EOI partners in the event that they do not think sufficient information has been provided by the EOI partner in their request. Over the review period, Uruguay sent a request for further clarification

relating to eight EOI requests from two treaty partners. Officials from the DGI have reported that these clarifications were made with regards to details of the requests which were missing (such as specifying the invoices; etc.).

257. In addition, Section 9 of Decree No. 313/011 states that the same limitation period will apply to an incoming request for information as is applicable under the domestic laws of the requesting jurisdiction. This reflects the principle that a jurisdiction can decline to provide information which the requesting jurisdiction would not be able to obtain under its own laws. This provision appears to be in conformity with the international standard. In practice, this provision has not been applied during the peer-review period.

Gathering information in practice

258. A total of 17 direct tax requests were sent to Uruguay over the review period. Uruguay counts an EOI request as one request regardless of the number of entities for which information is requested. The following procedures are those in place by the DGI for accessing ownership, banking and accounting information.

Access to ownership information

259. The processes used by the DGI to access ownership information are described below.

Information gathered internally by the DGI

260. The DGI hold a large amount of information, which is available in its own databases. These are for example taxpayer's identity information, and transfer pricing information. The DGI maintains a taxpayer identification system referred to as *Sistema de Identificacion de Contribuyentes* (SIC). A search engine is embedded in the database, with information that can be retrieved easily by using criteria, such as the RUT of the taxpayer, name, date of birth, address, the name of the company or the social security number. Through this system the DGI can obtain a large amount of information regarding taxpayers. This database is used to retrieve the initial ownership information of companies. However, updated ownership information is only maintained in the case of a transfer of interest in personal companies (limited liability companies (SRL) and partnerships).

261. Further, the DGI also has direct access to the information held by other governmental databases such as the National Direction of Customs, the National Registries, certain information maintained by the BCU and the Ministry of Energy, Trademarks and Patents. Further, in regards to certain information held by the BCU, the DGI can access this information online

with the use of a token. Memorandums of Understandings have been signed between the DGI and the BCU. In case the information is not directly accessible by the DGI, the DGI has broad powers to request information from other governmental agencies. In such cases the government bodies are given a short time period to provide this information, which generally does not exceed 10 days.

Information gathered from other intergovernmental agencies

262. The Large Taxpayer Division of the DGI gathers the requested information in cases where it cannot be extracted from the DGI's database. If the information has to be requested from another section of the DGI, this will be done by means of a memorandum signed by the Director of the Large Taxpayer Division which will establish a deadline, depending on the complexity of the task. The memorandum will be submitted in an envelope stating that the request is "urgent" and "confidential", and informing all participating employees that confidentiality norms must be taken into consideration while processing the request.

263. Regarding cases where no deadlines have been set by regulations, the DGI has entered into intergovernmental agreements with entities that have information that may be subject to EOI, as described below:

- Central Bank of Uruguay (BCU): The DGI carries on regular communication with the BCU. They concluded a Memorandum of Understanding to establish a quick procedure to access information about the owners of bearer equity interests. The procedure consists of requesting information through an electronic system subject to rigorous confidentiality. This allows the DGI to access information within a two to three-day period. Contacts were also identified to facilitate communication and the processing of requests, as well as deal with any contingencies that may arise.
- Social Security Fund (BPS, *Banco de Previsión Social*): BPS is an autonomous entity which co-ordinates the State's retirement services and organises social security. BPS collects social security contributions, Retirement Taxes, and the National Health Fund. This entity's database can be accessed directly by the DGI with a personal password given to a reduced number of employees.
- General Office of Registries (DGR, in Spanish): The DGR is an executing entity of the Ministry of Education and Culture whose object is to record, certify and make public all acts, legal transactions and decisions made by competent authorities that are subject by law to publicity of registrations. This entity's database can be accessed directly with a personal password given to a reduced number of employees within the DGI.

- National Internal Audit (AIN, in spanish): The AIN is an executing entity of the Ministry of Economy and Finance which has a register of financial statements from business corporations, agricultural businesses and associations, co-operatives, and trust funds and investment funds not subject to the BCU's control. It also has a current register of bylaws from corporations, and it is in charge of verifying compliance with the system set forth in Law No. 18 930 (bearer shares). The AIN shall inform the DGI of any business corporations or entities that fail to comply with their reporting obligations, so that the DGI suspends the business clearance certificate. To that end, a co-operation agreement has been agreed on which establishes an electronic procedure to access such information.
- National Customs Office (DNA *Dirección Nacional de Aduanas*): This entity's database can be accessed directly with a personal password, with different clearance levels depending on the users.

264. Finally, when norms do not establish a deadline and no inter-institutional agreements have been subscribed, the Director of the Large Taxpayer Division gives the order to gather the information establishing a deadline to complete the process. During the peer review period, deadlines have not exceeded five business days, except for the procedure established for banking information, where a deadline of 3 working days was put in place in the 5 cases where the information was obtained directly from the bank account holder. The authorities of Uruguay have stated that, notwithstanding the fact that there is no mandatory legal deadline in these cases, it has been standard practice until now to provide the requested information quickly, taking into account the importance and urgency of the matter. In all cases, the Large Taxpayer Division follows up on the request to ensure the information is obtained within a reasonable period of time for the response to be sent to the requiring State in a timely manner.

Information gathered from the taxpayer

265. In cases where information is requested directly from the taxpayer, information will be gathered by means of a memorandum signed by the Director of the Large Taxpayer Division, which establishes a deadline, depending on the complexity of the information requested. So far, deadlines have not exceeded five business days, except for the procedure established for bank information, where a deadline of 3 working days is provided for voluntary disclosure.

266. No templates or model letters or resolutions exist for requests for information of taxpayers and/or third parties as such information is obtained personally from the taxpayer and/or third parties by officials of the Large

Taxpayer Division, Control and/or the DGI at the taxpayer's and/or third party's address. However, when the information is to be collected by officials outside the DGI, the Large Taxpayer Division has drafted a sample memorandum that is sent to the aforesaid officials, identifying the information requested and the steps to be taken to collect such information.

Information gathered from third parties

267. In case the information must be accessed from a third party pursuant to article 68 of the tax Code, the DGI has broad access and investigation powers. Under article 70 of the Tax Code, persons issued with a notice to produce information are obliged to produce it. In case of non-compliance they are subjected to sanctions. Over the review period, notices to produce information were delivered in person. This occurred eight times over the review period. A summoning letter, which is issued to the third party, specifies the information required by the DGI. The Uruguayan authorities have clarified that they never state the reason for the summons or the agreement under which it is required. During the peer review period, this summoning letter has been either delivered by a member of the EOI Unit or an auditor from the large taxpayer unit (when the requested information concerned companies) or an auditor from the small taxpayer department.

268. Over the review period, the EOI Unit received the support of the police, but only with respect to domestic tax cases, and not for EOI purposes. Similarly, over the review period, search and seizure warrants were issued seven times, but all for domestic tax purposes. The Authorities of Uruguay have confirmed that they would request the support of the police in EOI cases, should that be necessary.

Use of information gathering measures absent domestic tax interest (ToR B.1.3)

269. The concept of "domestic tax interest" describes a situation where a contracting party can only access information for EOI purposes, if it also has an interest in the requested information for its own tax purposes. Uruguay has advised that the access powers available to the DGI under domestic law are not curtailed by a domestic tax interest and may be used to access information sought in an EOI request.

Compulsory powers *(ToR B.1.4)*

270. For information that is not already held by the DGI or publicly available, the DGI may use its access powers to obtain ownership, identity and accounting information that is under the custody or control of an individual

or entity for the purposes of satisfying a specific exchange of information request. The powers include, but are not limited to, making inquiries, carrying out inspections, and the search and seizure of documents. The Uruguayan authorities did not have to apply compulsory powers during the peer review period,

271. Non-compliance with access powers carries significant penalties: for refusing to provide information or hindering the actions of a tax official, the DGI may impose administrative penalties of between UYU 240 and UYU 5.640 (USD 10 to USD 235) for 2014 (USD 1: UYU 24). Where a person is in contempt (including open disobedience with an official's orders), penal sanctions of 3-18months imprisonment may apply (article 173, Criminal Code).

272. With respect to obtaining bank information under the process described below in Section B.1.5, a financial institution that fails to comply with a request from the Central Bank is punishable by the Central Bank. The sanctions imposed under article 20 of Decree Law 15 322 can include a written warning, fines, management intervention, an order to suspend activities, or revocation of their authorisation from the BCU to carry out financial intermediation activities. In the case of the revocation of the authorisation to operate, this is imposed by the Superintendent of Financial Services (FSB), an office that is linked to the Central Bank. No sanctions have been imposed during the peer review period.

Secrecy provisions *(ToR B.1.5)*

273. Professional secrecy, which includes bank secrecy, is protected by the Uruguayan Constitution (Article 7)[28], which allows exceptions where a specific law so provides and it is "established for reasons of public interest". There is no specific legislation regarding the duty of confidentiality of non-financial professions (including lawyers and notaries). However, the Administrative Law Court (*Tribunal en lo Contencioso Administrativo*

28. Article 7 of the Constitution provides the following: "The inhabitants of the Republic have a right to be protected regarding their entitlement to life, honor, freedom, security work and property. No one can be denied these rights but for the laws established for reasons of general interest". The Constitution does not expressly mention professional secrecy and in particular bank secrecy. However, in Uruguay professional secrecy, including bank secrecy, are deemed to be covered by these constitutional rights pursuant to article 72 of the Constitution: "The express provision for rights, duties and guarantees made under this Constitution does not exclude the other fundamental rights inherent to human nature or derived from the republican way of government".

– TCA) has issued two decisions[29] in which it was decided that professional secrecy cannot be invoked by an accountant as a valid defense against the tax authorities. Uruguay does not have any judicial precedent regarding notaries or any other non-financial professions, but the same solutions as found in the above mentioned court cases can be expected. In addition, Uruguay has confirmed that they have not encountered any issue regarding professional secrecy in their administrative practice. The secrecy of bank information (article 25, Decree Law 15 322) and information held by trustees (article 19(c), Trusts Law) is underscored by specific domestic legislation.

274. Over the review period, Uruguay received ten EOI requests related to banking information. In practice, banking information was gathered only in five cases where it was accessed directly from the taxpayer, as noted under section A.3 above on the *Availability of Banking Information* and detailed in this section below. In no cases did claims of bank secrecy or other secrecy provisions prevent access to information.

Bank Secrecy

275. Decree Law 15 322 imposes an obligation of secrecy to certain activities carried out by any person performing financial intermediation activities (articles 1 and 2, with article 25). In particular, article 25 states that banks cannot reveal any "confidential" information which has been received from their clients or in respect of them while article 1 and 2 of Decree Law 15 322 describe the scope of the article 25 secrecy obligation. That is, bank secrecy applies to persons carrying out financial intermediation in respect of any confidential information received from the customer-related operations, including where the account holder is a creditor of the financial intermediary.

276. Further, Decree Law 15 322 specifically states that "no other exception than those set forth in this act will be admitted". Failure to observe the requirements of bank secrecy under article 25 carries a penalty of a minimum 3 months and maximum of 3 years imprisonment.

277. There are some cases where bank secrecy can be lifted to access bank information for the purposes of an EOI request. Law 18 718 passed in December 2010 and entering into force from 2 January 2011 amends article 54 of the Tax Reform Law 18 083 and permits the lifting of bank secrecy as required by an EOI agreement (article 15(2), Law 18 718)[30]:

---

29. TCA, N° 342/2007 and N° 599/2012.
30. Article 15(1) also provides for the lifting of professional secrecy for domestic purposes when it is necessary for the determination of tax debts or concerning the breach of tax obligations, if there are objective pieces of evidence creating a reasonable doubt about a tax evasion purpose of the taxpayer. However, that

> 15(2) It [bank secrecy] may also be lifted anytime where there is a request from the Tax Administration Agency, asking for access to information in order to respond to a foreign tax Administration Agency with which there is an agreement in place for information exchange or to avoid double taxation.

This exception for banking information in the case of EOI requests applies to account information from 2 January 2011. As concerns this scope, none of Uruguay's EOI agreements (with the exception of its DTCs with Germany, Hungary, and Mexico and its TIEA with France) entered into force prior to 2 January 2011. However, a transaction may occur prior to 2 January 2011, but relate to a tax period relevant under an EOI agreement, and that bank information would not be accessible. Therefore, in a limited number of requests, this limitation will pose an impediment to accessing bank information and a Phase 1 recommendation is made in this respect.

278. The Tax Reform Law clearly provides an exception to the bank secrecy established by article 25 of Decree Law 15 322, but that article also states that only the exceptions stated "therein" shall apply. Therefore in creating the exception it may have been advisable to directly amend Decree Law 15 322, or at least include a reference to the exceptions contained in the Tax Reform Law. However the intent to allow access to bank information in the case of an EOI requests is clear.[31] In terms of overriding the constitutional protection for professional secrecy, it is clear that Tax Reform Law is a "specific law" and that the purpose of giving effect to Uruguay's information exchange provisions is a "reason of public interest".

279. In addition to the exception to bank secrecy for EOI purposes, there are also several exceptions for access for domestic law purposes, for example where the consent of the person concerned is given or it is required by a court order for use in proceedings (Decree Law 15 322), as well as in respect of proceedings relating to rental discounts concerning the financial situation of the tenant (Law 15 799) and in respect of reports of suspicious transactions under the anti-money laundering regime (Laws 17 835 and 18 494).

---

provision only permits the use of the information by the judge to determine the tax evasion charges.

31. Similar exceptions have existed for criminal proceedings and family law matters for some time (see below). Further, article 28 of the Criminal Code provides an exemption from liability where an act is sanctioned by the law: "A person who executes an act ordered or allowed by law, because of his public functions, profession or his authority or the provision of assistance to a judicial authority, is exempt from responsibility.".

Availability of banking information in practice

280. According to the wording given by Article 15 of Law No. 18 718 and regulatory decree No. 282/011, amending Law No. 18 083, the first step to obtain this information is to request the bank account holders if they will willingly lift bank secrecy. Once notified of the request, the person has five business days to express their will.

281. Two situations may arise:

- The bank account holder authorises the lifting of bank secrecy. In that case, the DGI will send the BCU a copy of the authorisation. The BCU will then have five business days starting from the day after receiving the authorisation to notify the bank's authorities of the DGI's request for information. The notified banks must provide the requested information within 15 business days from notification and, once the deadline is reached, the BCU has five business days to provide the information it collected to the DGI. It should be noted however that the request for the voluntary disclosure of information protected by bank secrecy applies prior to the request for judicial lifting of bank secrecy, except for the cases listed below[32], in which lifting of bank secrecy can only be requested judicially:
    - Taxpayers whose home address has not been filed at the DGI (this includes non-resident individuals and companies);
    - Persons with Uruguayan tax liability;
    - Individuals or legal persons that can be used to conceal the identity of the true bank account holders; and
    - Individuals or entities that do not pay the taxes administered by the DGI.
- In the case that the bank account holder does not voluntary authorise the lifting of bank secrecy within the five-day period, the DGI can request a Judge to lift bank secrecy within ten business days of the expiration of the five-day period (see details in paragraphs 305-307). The law establishes a simplified judicial procedure to lift bank secrecy. Once bank secrecy is lifted, the BCU is informed and the same procedure and deadlines, as in the case of voluntary lifting of bank secrecy, will apply.

282. With respect to cases of non-voluntary disclosures, the litigation department of the DGI works in collaboration with the legal unit of the BCU. Since the entry into force of the amendments to Law No. 18 083, a joint team was created

32. Section A.4.3.1.1 of Resolution N° 1774/2014.

with attorneys and special guidelines were prepared for the collaboration with judges. For each request, a file is created under confidentiality. The BCU has five days to inform the DGI of the responses obtained from the bank. Where the institutions (banks) fail to provide the information, the BCU can impose a penalty. This took place in only one instance, which was not EOI related.

283. During the peer review period, banking information was exchanged in 5 cases but the provisions on direct access to bank information were not used to do so (as the information was provided by the taxpayer). The first case of directly accessing bank information from the banks for EOI purposes took place after the peer review period.

284. In one case where the information was not provided, the information requested to the DGI dated back more than ten years. The DGI attempted to gather the banking information from the taxpayer, but was unable to retrieve the information for multiple reasons; one of them being that the taxpayer had passed away one year before the request was made. Under the standard, it is not required that the bank information be available for more than 5 years, but it is required that if the information is available (for example with a bank), the information be accessed by the Uruguayan authorities. However, due to the bank secrecy law which cannot be lifted for banking information prior to 2 January 2011, the DGI was unable to access information from the bank dated back 2000.

285. The provisions of Law No. 18 718 remained untested in practice during the peer review period. It should be noted however that the judicial procedure has been tested after the peer review period, with eight successful cases, as at 1 July 2014. However, these cases did not concern information on transactions prior to 2 January 2011. The Uruguayan authorities are recommended to monitor the application of Law 18 718 to the access and exchange of banking information,

Secrecy of information held by trustees

286. Uruguayan law also protects the confidentiality of information held by trustees. Article 19(c) of the Trusts Law provides that:

> 19(c). In addition to the obligations established in the trust instrument and the articles above, the trustee shall…not disclose any transaction, act, contract, document and information relating to the trust

287. However, where the trust is subject to tax in Uruguay, the trustee is responsible for the trust's tax obligations (articles 36 and 44, Trusts Law). Therefore, the DGI's access powers will apply to allow it to access the information held by trustee in those instances.

288. Until 2012, where the trustee was located in Uruguay but the trust was not subject to tax there (noting its largely territorial tax system), there did not appear to be a mechanism to lift trustee confidentiality where the information was sought for EOI purposes. In Uruguay's view, access to such information was possible in such cases under article 68E of the Tax Code, in order to establish that the trust was not subject to tax. However, the information required to establish that there was no Uruguayan source income, did not appear to require a disclosure of all relevant information relating to the trust.

289. The law was amended to ensure, in cases where a trust is not subject to Uruguayan tax and is managed by a Uruguayan trustee, access to information regarding that trust when sought for EOI purposes. Section 19 of Law No. 18 930 states that: "The trustee confidentiality duty established under c), article 19 of Act 17 703, as of October 27, 2003, shall not be effective against the DGI and the BCU." This provision expressly overrides the confidentiality provision described above with respect to disclosure of information to the Uruguayan tax authorities, both for domestic and EOI purposes, and regardless of the tax status of the trust.

290. In practice, officials from the DGI have reported and peer input confirms that to date Uruguay has not received any EOI requests relating to a trust. In the event that Uruguay were to receive an EOI request concerning ownership or identity information pertaining to a trust, they do not envisage any issues with accessing this information from a trustee.

Determination and factors underlying recommendations

Phase 1 Determination	
The element is in place, but certain aspects of its legal implementation need improvement.	
Factors underlying recommendations	**Recommendations**
Uruguay's ability to access bank information prior to 2 January 2011 is limited under its domestic legislation.	Uruguay should ensure that all relevant bank information may be accessed for EOI purposes, regardless of the period to which the information relates, to ensure they can give full effect to their EOI agreements.

Phase 2 Rating	
Partially compliant	
Factors underlying recommendations	**Recommendations**
During the peer review period, Uruguay did not gather banking information from banks concerning information on transactions taking place before 2 January 2011 for exchange of information purposes. In addition, Uruguay did not gather banking information from banks concerning information on transactions taking place after 2 January 2011, although it has done so after the peer review period. Accordingly, the effectiveness of the access powers could not be assessed.	Uruguay should ensure that all relevant bank information may be accessed for exchange of information purposes and monitor the implementation of the access powers in practice.

B.2. Notification requirements and rights and safeguards

The rights and safeguards (e.g. notification, appeal rights) that apply to persons in the requested jurisdiction should be compatible with effective exchange of information.

Not unduly prevent or delay exchange of information (ToR B.2.1)

Prior notification requirements

291. Uruguay has brought into force Decree No. 313/011 which sets the procedure for exchange of information by Uruguay, under its DTCs and TIEAs. Amongst other things, this Decree provides for a prior notification requirement in the context of responding to EOI requests received by Uruguay. Section 10 of Decree No. 313/011 states that:

> "No decision shall be made to submit information to a requesting competent authority without granting the prior notification to the person the information corresponds for five business days."

292. This appeared to require prior notification to all cases of exchange of information by Uruguay, not only in cases involving bank information (see below). No exception to this requirement was set out in Decree No. 313/011. Under Section 10 of Decree No. 313/011, prior notification had to be given to the person who is subject to investigation or examination in the requesting

jurisdiction (i.e. the taxpayer). It is noted that, in all cases, it appeared no decision regarding whether to respond to an incoming EOI request could be made by the DGI until such notification has been given.

293. Uruguay issued Decree N° 378/2013 on 26 November 2013 amended Article 10 as follows:

> "Prior to sending the information collected, the competent authority or an authorised representative thereof, shall allow the individuals or entities being reviewed or audited in the requesting State to access such information for a five-working-day period as long as such individuals or entities have established and registered their address with the DGI"

294. Prior to this change, the Uruguayan authorities interpreted Article 10 of Decree No. 313/011, such that prior notification had to be made to the person concerned by the request, whether or not resident in Uruguay. Even though prior notification was carried out, none of the persons notified sought to check the file during or after the peer review period. The letter of notification included an invitation for the notified person to check his/her file within five working days at the DGI. The file does not include the letter of request. In substance, the file contains only the information that the DGI include in the response to the request and does not disclose the name of the requesting jurisdiction. This notification, which has a suspensive effect only for five days, does not give any statutory rights to the taxpayer.

295. Since November 2013, the notification is only sent to persons who are being investigated in another jurisdiction and who have registered their home address with the DGI. This means that for example a non-resident individual having solely a bank account in Uruguay would not be notified of the request. Since the authorities have introduced this new interpretation of Article 10 of Decree No 313/011, no notification has taken place in practice, as all requests related to persons not having registered their address with the DGI.

Prior notification in practice

296. The notification to the taxpayer always takes place after the information has been gathered, but prior to its exchange. This procedure has been established to comply with the provision set out in Article 66 of the Constitution under which information must be given on all administrative process for the due process of law.

297. During the peer review period, no taxpayers presented themselves to the DGI to view their file resulting from the prior notification procedure. One peer reported that it had to withdraw a request after being notified by Uruguay of the prior notification procedure set out in Article 10 of Decree

No. 313/011, and the absence of exceptions to this procedure. It is therefore recommended that Uruguay sets out that suitable exceptions from the prior notification requirement are permitted to facilitate effective exchange of information (e.g. in cases in which the information requested is of a very urgent nature or the notification is likely to undermine the chance of the success of the investigation conducted by the requesting jurisdiction).

298. The compulsory notification requirement under Article 10 of Decree No. 313/011 combined with the lack of clear exceptions from this requirement has the potential to unduly prevent or delay effective exchange of information and also may undermine the chance of the success of the investigation conducted by the requesting jurisdiction. Accordingly, it is recommended that clarification on the application of suitable exceptions from this prior notification requirement be provided.

Access to banking information

299. In the case of accessing information subject to bank secrecy, a written request to a court is required, guided by the provisions of the Tax Reform Law and the General Code of Proceedings which applies for non-penal proceedings in Uruguay. The proceedings are confidential to persons with an interest in the proceedings.

300. Under Law 18 083, modified by Law 18 718 (Article 15) the DGI first makes a written request to the Court to issue a writ, which should be done (article 54, Tax Reform Law):

> "pursuant to express and well-grounded requests by the competent authority of a foreign state… and it must be indicated in such case the requiring entity and all the records and grounds that justify the relevance of the requested information".

301. The request and the writ issued by the Court to access the information shall be advised to the account-holder (often, being the taxpayer the subject of the request, or their proxy) within 3 working days of its issue. The account-holder has 6 business days to respond, including by way of providing the requested information. The matter should be listed for hearing within 30 calendar days from the response.[33]

302. The judge will make an order determining whether to lift bank secrecy, taking into consideration "the collected evidence and all the circumstances of the case". Uruguay has advised that the purpose of the judicial review is to consider the legality of the request (that is, that the condition set out in the

33. Whether a hearing is necessary shall depend on the extent of the information which may have been provided, or where the judge seeks clarification of any issues.

TIEA have been met), rather than for example to make any determination of the relevance of the information requested or the merits of the investigation. To the extent that this consideration does not appear to extend to a determination of the "foreseeable relevance" of the request, it is consistent with the standard.

303. After a judgement is passed, the decision is appealable with suspensive effect, to the Civil Court of Appeals. This process involves 18 business days between the appellation and response. The Court must rule within 30 days of receiving the court file. There is no further appeal beyond the Civil Court of Appeals. Once the order has been made and appeals exhausted, a notice is issued to the BCU as the supervisory entity for all financial institutions. Within 5 business days, the Central Bank must submit the request to all entities subject to its supervision. Those entities then have 15 business days to send relevant information in their possession to the Central Bank, and the Central Bank has another 5 business days to send the information to the DGI.

304. Noting the possibility of appeal, the Uruguayan authorities have advised that the timeline for access to bank information may be up to 180 days. This procedure was not used during the peer review period, as in all cases where banking information was provided, this was submitted to the DGI by the taxpayer, such that there was no requirement for the DGI to utilise this court procedure. However, for the procedures which took place after the peer review period, the timeline for access to bank information in case of non-voluntary disclosure amounted to 180 days in average. The timeline is expected to get shorter as the judges become increasingly familiar with the procedure.

305. Two issues which may be inconsistent with the standard arise from this court process. First, there are no exceptions to the obligation of prior notification of the account-holder. Second, the court process to access bank information raises an issue of consistency with Uruguay's confidentiality obligations under each of its EOI agreements that may arise where the account-holder is not the taxpayer or their proxy. This is considered further in section C.3 *Confidentiality* of the report.

Exception to prior notification in banking

306. The legislation requires that "all the records and grounds" must be disclosed to the court and the relevant account-holder as party to those proceedings will be privy to all of that information. Whilst the standard provides that the fact that information is being exchange may be disclosed to the taxpayer (or their proxy), exceptions to limit that notification prior to the information being exchanged should be in place, to apply for example in situations where the request was of a very urgent nature or such disclosure would compromise the investigation being concluded in the requesting State.

307. Uruguay has advised that in its view, the general provisions of the General Procedural Code will apply to create an appropriate exception, because they permit an ex-parte application to the Court in appropriate cases. Uruguay has advised that the abovementioned notification may be delayed by the DGI in case of urgency, in order to safeguard evidence that could be destroyed or to find out information regarding a taxpayer that could leave the country, through application to the court for a preventative measure order (under s. 311 of the General Procedure Code). Whilst Uruguayan case law suggests that this preventative measure can be invoked by the DGI in the context of preventing the disclosure of information to a person in the context of domestic tax proceedings, it is not clear that the preventative measures under s. 311 of the General Procedure Code may be relied upon in the EOI context. It is also not clear that this Code will overrule the clear and specific provisions for the judicial process to access bank information due to the "latter in time" rule. Further, even if the General Procedural Code does apply to create an exception, its provisions do not appear to apply to prevent notification prior to the information being exchanged, only in respect of preventing notification prior to the information being accessed, and thus in any event would still not be consistent with the standard.

308. The possibility of an exception under article 311 (as outlined above) has never been applied in practice in an EOI case. Should the requirement for it arise, the DGI has confirmed that it would go to a judge and ask to have access to banking information in which case it would have to demonstrate the right to request the information and the possible harm that notification would entail. Officials from the Attorney General Office have reported that in such instance, the decision of the judge would be predicated on two Latin maxims that form the basis of the legal system; *fumus bonis juris* (to be in the right spirit of the law) and the other being *periculum in mora* (danger in delay if the judge does not concede to abrogating the prior notification procedure). Although Uruguay has not as yet had any requirement to use this procedure for domestic or EOI purposes, officials have reported they would not foresee any issues applying this procedure to postpone notifications until after the information has been accessed.

309. Nevertheless, considering the absence of express exceptions to prior notification in the law and given the absence of cases in which s. 311 of the General Procedure Code was applied, Uruguay should ensure that disclosure of information relating to an EOI request in the course of a Court process to access bank information includes appropriate exceptions to notifications prior to exchange of information.

Conclusion

310. The two notification procedures set out under Uruguyan law do not provide for any exceptions (e.g. in cases in which the information requested is of a very urgent nature or the notification is likely to undermine the chance of success of the investigation conducted by the requesting jurisdiction). In addition to ensuring appropriate exceptions to notification prior to exchange of information, the Uruguayan authorities should continue to closely monitor that these prior notification procedures do not affect exchange of information in practice. In light of the deficiencies identified in the legal framework of Uruguay regarding the absence of exceptions to the two prior notification procedures, the overall rating for element B.2 is determined as "Partially Compliant".

Determination and factors underlying recommendations

Phase 1 Determination	
The element is in place, but certain aspects of the legal implementation of the element need improvement.	
Factors underlying recommendations	**Recommendations**
Under the court process for accessing bank information, certain information must be provided to the Uruguayan court to which the relevant account-holder (often the taxpayer) will have access. There are no exceptions to this notification of the account-holder prior to exchange of information, for example for cases where the information requested is of a very urgent nature, or where praior notification is likely to undermine the chance of success of the investigation in the requesting jurisdiction.	Uruguay should ensure that disclosure of information relating to an EOI request in the course of the court process to access bank information includes appropriate exceptions to notification prior to exchange of the information.
Decree no. 313/011, as amended, requires the prior notification of the individual or entity concerned prior to the tax authority's decision on responding to an incoming EOI request. It is not clear that there are appropriate exceptions from this prior notification procedure.	It is recommended that Uruguay clarifies that suitable exceptions from the prior notification requirement are permitted to facilitate effective exchange of information (e.g. in cases in which the information requested is of a very urgent nature or the notification is likely to undermine the chance of success of the investigation conducted by the requesting jurisdiction).

Phase 2 Rating
Partially compliant

C. Exchanging Information

Overview

311. Jurisdictions generally cannot exchange information for tax purposes unless they have a legal basis or mechanism for doing so. In Uruguay, the legal authority to exchange information derives from bilateral mechanisms (double tax conventions) as well as from domestic law. This section of the report examines whether Uruguay has a network of information exchange that would allow it to achieve effective exchange of information in practice. The 31 EOI agreements concluded by Uruguay to date generally follow the OECD Model Double Tax Convention (DTC) or Model Tax Information Exchange Agreement (Model TIEA) respectively. Prior to 2012, provisions in domestic law concerning information held by trustees could impede Uruguay's ability to give full effect to those agreements. This issue has been fully addressed by Law No. 18 930 as described in Section B.1 of this report.

312. Uruguay has, since 2009, begun to sign an increasing number of EOI agreements. It has ratified and brought into force DTCs with Finland, Germany, Korea, India, Liechtenstein, Malta, Mexico, Ecuador, Romania, Portugal, Spain and Switzerland. Further, it has signed a DTC with Belgium, United Arab Emirates and Vietnam, which are not yet in force Uruguay has also concluded an additional 15 EOI agreements, eight of which are in force, which generally follow the OECD Model Tax Convention or Model TIEA respectively, as further examined under this section. Uruguay signed two TIEAs in 2011 and two TIEAs in 2012, which are not yet in force. However, Uruguay has taken all of the steps necessary to bring the TIEAs signed in 2011 into force, except for the TIEAs signed in 2012. Element C.1 is determined "in place".

313. During the review period, information was not exchanged in eight cases concerning criminal tax matters and in 4 civil tax matters due to a specific interpretation by Uruguay of the entry into force provision of its TIEA with Argentina. The interpretation by Uruguay of the entry into force of the TIEA concluded with Argentina is not in line with the international standard. Element C.1 has been determined "in place" but as a result of the interpretative issue is rated "largely compliant'.

314. At the beginning of 2011, Uruguay did not have an EOI agreement with two of its major trading partners (Argentina and Brazil) which requested to enter into treaty negotiations with Uruguay at that time. Uruguay has made significant progress in expanding its network and concluded a TIEA with both of its major trading partners. The TIEA with Argentina entered into force on 7 February 2013, whereas ratification of the TIEA with Brazil is still pending on both sides. Accordingly, element C.2 is determined "in place" and rated "compliant".

315. The confidentiality provisions in Uruguay's domestic laws and EOI agreements generally support the confidentiality of information in line with the requirements of the international standard. In addition, effective measures and procedures have been put in place to ensure confidentiality of information in practice. Accordingly, element C.3 is found to be in place and is rated Compliant.

316. Rights and safeguards for taxpayers and third parties (element C.4) are protected under Uruguay's agreements consistently with the international standard. Before 2012, the parameters of legal privilege under Uruguayan law could not be clearly determined under element C.4. Uruguay has introduced new provisions which bring more certainty with respect to ownership information held by trustees and on ownership information concerning bearer shares and foreign companies. Uruguay has also provided court decisions and further explanation on the scope of the professional secrecy provision. As a result, the determination under Element C.4 is "the element is in place" and the rating is "compliant".

317. During the period under review (July 2010 – June 2013), Uruguay received 17 requests related to income tax from four jurisdictions[34]. Out of the 17 requests, Uruguay provided the requested information in only 5 cases due to the divergence of interpretation in the entry into force of one TIEA concluded with Argentina (see section C.1.9 *Be given effect through domestic law*). Uruguay created an EOI Unit within the DGI. The resources were increased by allocating staff and drafting an EOI Manual which sets out EOI procedures. The operational process also improved with experience.

318. As Uruguay processed only five income tax EOI requests during the three-year period under review, the organisational processes have not been sufficiently tested in practice. Accordingly, it is recommended that Uruguay keeps monitoring the practical implementation of the organisational processes of the competent authority. In addition, Uruguay did not provide an update or status report to its EOI partners within 90 days when the competent

34. In addition, during the peer review period, Uruguay received an additional amount of 12 requests related to VAT matters, which are not considered for the purpose of this report.

authority was not able to provide a substantive response within that time, unless it was specifically requested by the treaty partner. Uruguayshould ensure that updates to EOI partners are provided within 90 days in those cases where it is not possible to provide a partial or complete response within that timeframe. As a result, Element C.5 is rated "largely compliant".

C.1. Exchange-of-information mechanisms

Exchange of information mechanisms should allow for effective exchange of information.

319. The competent authority for the international exchange of tax information in Uruguay is the Ministry of Economy and Finance (MEF) or its duly authorised representative, as stated in exchange of information agreements concluded by Uruguay and as set out in Article 1 of Decree No. 313/011, dated September 2, 2011. Article 2 of Decree No. 313/011 authorises the MEF to delegate the competent authority duties to the DGI, including entering into memorandums of understanding, and receiving, evaluating and processing exchange requests. By virtue of Resolutions by the Executive Branch dated August 11, 2011, and September 19, 2013, the MEF delegated its powers as competent authority to the DGI for matters related to exchange of information under Decree 313/011.

320. In turn, the General Revenue Director of the MEF delegated to the Deputy Director General, the Director of the Large Taxpayer Division, and the Head of the International Taxation Department his capacity as competent authority. Within the DGI, the Director General's Office and the Large Taxpayer Division (International Taxation Department) are involved in managing exchanges of information, and where necessary the Control Division and the Technical and Legal Division may also assist in the EOI process.

321. Since 2011, Uruguay has ratified and brought into force DTCs with Finland, Germany, Korea, India, Liechtenstein, Malta, Mexico, Portugal and Switzerland. Uruguay has also signed a DTC with Belgium, and Viet Nam, which are not yet in force and has concluded an additional 13 EOI agreements, ten of which are in force, which generally follow the OECD Model Tax Convention or Model Tax Information Exchange Agreement (OECD Model TIEA) respectively.

322. Over the peer review period, Uruguay has received requests from 5 jurisdictions.

Foreseeably relevant standard (ToR C.1.1)

323. The international standard for exchange of information envisages information exchange to the widest possible extent. Nevertheless it does not

allow "fishing expeditions" i.e. speculative requests for information that have no apparent nexus to an open inquiry or investigation. The balance between these two competing considerations is captured in the standard of "foreseeable relevance" which is included in article 1 of the OECD Model TIEA, as well as paragraph 1 of Article 26 of the OECD Model Taxation Convention which is set out below:

> The competent authorities of the contracting states shall exchange such information as is foreseeably relevant to the carrying out of the provisions of this convention or to the administration or enforcement of the domestic laws concerning taxes of every kind and description imposed on behalf of the contracting states or their political subdivisions or local authorities in so far as the taxation thereunder is not contrary to the Convention. The exchange of information is not restricted by Articles 1 and 2.

324. Uruguay has advised that it now seeks to include this paragraph or words to its effect (or its equivalent found in Article 1 of the OECD Model TIEA) in all of its EOI agreements. It is presently included in each of its 20 signed EOI agreements.[35]

325. The new DTCs with Korea and Finland, as well as the seven additional TIEAs with Argentina, Denmark, Faroe Islands, Greenland, Iceland, Norway and Sweden provide for the exchange of information that is "foreseeably relevant" to the administration and enforcement of the domestic tax laws of the contracting parties. In addition, the TIEA with Argentina explicitly states under Article 2(4) that "fishing expeditions" are not allowed under this EOI agreement.

Assessment of foreseeable relevance in practice

326. The assessment guidelines to determine whether or not a request for information is valid have been set forth in points A.1 to A.3, Chapter IV of the Procedure for the Effective International Exchange of Information on Request (the Guidelines), approved by Resolution N° 1774/2014 of the Director General.

327. Under these Guidelines, a procedure to check the validity of a request has been established. A preliminary formal assessment is first conducted regarding the elements included in the request, following the lists included in Article 5(5) of the Model TIEA. With respect to the assessment of the

35. In Uruguay's DTC with Hungary (entering into force in 1993), the EOI provision requires exchange of information as is "*necessary* to the carrying out…". Uruguay has confirmed that it interprets "necessary" consistently with the concept of foreseeable relevance.

substance of the request, a report is prepared and submitted to the consideration of the MEF in the cases listed below:

(i) when the information furnished might disclose commercial, managerial, industrial or professional secrets, commercial procedures or when it contains information whose disclosure to the competent Authority of the requesting State might contravene public order.

(ii) information concerning requests to authorise officials of the requesting competent authority to enter the national territory in order to interview individuals or review documents.

(iii) when presence at an audit in the national territory is implied in the request for exchange of information.

328. The Guidelines do not provide an explicit definition of foreseeable relevance. Instead it is stated that: "The 'foreseeable relevance' standard refers to the fact that the information to be exchanged is to be foreseeably relevant so that the provisions in the agreements in force be applicable or so that the tax provisions in the national law of the States bound by the agreements concerning any and all taxes collected by the aforesaid States, the political divisions or local entities thereof be enforced as long as such enforcement does not contravene the agreement." In practice, Uruguay has never declined a direct EOI tax request on the basis of lack of foreseeable relevance[36].

In respect of all persons (ToR C.1.2)

329. For exchange of information to be effective it is necessary that a jurisdiction's obligation to provide information is not restricted by the residence or nationality of the person to whom the information relates or by the residence or nationality of the person in possession or control of the information requested. For this reason the international standard envisages that exchange of information mechanisms will provide for exchange of information in respect of all persons.

330. None of Uruguay's EOI agreements are restricted for EOI purposes by the "persons covered" article in the DTC (equivalent to Article 1 of the OECD Model Convention). The DTCs with Belgium, Korea and Finland, as

36. In practice, Uruguay has refused to provide ownership information in 5 VAT cases, where the main inquiries in the requests concerned the veracity of invoices, on the ground that ownership information in these VAT cases were not foreseeably relevant. The Uruguayan authorities provided the information regarding the invoices, but it considered that the identity of the shareholders of the trading Uruguayan company was not foreseeably relevant. These cases have not been evaluated for the purposes of this report.

well as the seven TIEAs with Argentina, Australia, Canada, Denmark, Faroe Islands, Greenland, Iceland, Norway and Sweden provide for EOI in respect of all persons.

331. In practice, both discussions with the Uruguayan authorities and feedback from EOI partners indicate that no difficulties have arisen with any of its exchange of information partners regarding an exchange request relating to residents of either of the contracting states or residents of third party jurisdictions.

Obligation to exchange all types of information (ToR C.1.3)

332. Jurisdictions cannot engage in effective exchange of information if they cannot exchange information held by financial institutions, nominees or persons acting in an agency or a fiduciary capacity. Both the OECD Model Convention and the Model Agreement on Exchange of Information which are the authoritative sources of the standards, stipulate that bank secrecy cannot form the basis for declining a request to provide information and that a request for information cannot be declined solely because the information is held by nominees or persons acting in an agency or fiduciary capacity or because the information relates to an ownership interest.

333. The DTCs with Belgium, Ecuador, Finland, India, Korea, Liechtenstein, Malta, Mexico, Portugal, Romania, Spain and Viet Nam contain a provision that mirrors Article 26(5) of the OECD Model Tax Convention spelling out the obligations of the contracting parties to exchange information held by financial institutions, nominees, agents and ownership and identity information. Likewise, a provision equivalent to Article 5(4) of the OECD Model TIEA establishing such obligation is found in each of Uruguay's TIEAs. However, Uruguay's DTC with Hungary (signed in 1988) does not include such a provision.

334. Uruguay has advised it interprets its DTCs with Hungary so as not to limit the exchange of information held by financial institutions, nominees or persons acting in a fiduciary capacity. However, the limitations of its domestic law would appear to remain. In particular, the exchange of information which is subject to bank secrecy to the extent it relates to transactions occurring prior to 2 January 2011 will still be limited under that DTC to instances where the person concerned gives written permission to disclose the information.[37]

335. Prior to 2012, all the EOI agreements signed by Uruguay were subject to the apparent restriction on access to information held by trustees in respect of certain trusts, which was considered inconsistent with the standard.

37. This "written permission" exception is found in Decree Law 15 322.

As explained under Section B.1. of this report, article 19(c) of the Trusts Law imposed a confidentiality obligation upon trustees with regard to transactions, acts, contracts, documents and information relating to the trust. This obligation was not clearly overridden by article 68E of the Tax Code where no Uruguayan income was derived through the trust. Nevertheless, Uruguay has adequately addressed the issue through introduction of an express override to trustee confidentiality under Section 19 of Law No. 18 930.

Absence of domestic tax interest (ToR C.1.4)

336. The concept of "domestic tax interest" describes a situation where a contracting party can only provide information to another contracting party if it has an interest in the requested information for its own tax purposes. An inability to provide information based on a domestic tax interest requirement is not consistent with the international standard. Contracting parties must use their information gathering measures even though invoked solely to obtain and provide information to the other contracting party.

337. Uruguay's DTC with Hungary does not include a provision equivalent to Article 26(4) of the OECD Model Convention which expressly precludes the application of a domestic tax interest. However, as with its other EOI agreements, this does not impede Uruguay's use of domestic access powers in respect of requests made under those DTCs.

338. The DTCs with Belgium, Ecuador, Finland, India, Korea, Liechtenstein, Malta, Mexico, Portugal, Romania, Spain and Viet Nam contain a provision equivalent to Article 26(4) of the OECD Model Tax Convention, which obliges the Contracting Parties to use their information gathering measures to obtain and provide information to the requesting jurisdiction even in cases where the requested Party does not have a domestic interest in the requested information. Similarly, a provision corresponding to Article 5(2) of the OECD Model TIEA establishing such obligation is included in each of the TIEAs signed by Uruguay.

Absence of dual criminality principles (ToR C.1.5)

339. The principle of dual criminality provides that assistance can only be provided if its conduct being investigated (and giving rise to an information request) would constitute a crime under the laws of the requested country if it had occurred in the requested country. In order to be effective, exchange of information should not be constrained by the application of the dual criminality principle.

340. There are no dual criminality provisions in Uruguay's EOI agreements. Uruguay's policy in this regard is to exchange information under its

agreements irrespective of whether the conduct being investigated would constitute a crime in Uruguay.

341. Uruguayan authorities have reported and peer input confirms that no request has been turned down on this basis during the period under review.

Exchange of information in both civil and criminal tax matters (ToR C.1.6)

342. Information exchange may be requested both for tax administration purposes and for tax prosecution purposes. The international standard is not limited to information exchange in criminal tax matters but extends to information requested for tax administration purposes (also referred to as "civil tax matters"). Each of Uruguay's EOI agreements provides for exchange of information in both civil and criminal tax matters.

343. Out of the seventeen requests sent to Uruguay during the three-year review period, Uruguay did not provide information requested to Argentina on criminal tax matters in eight cases. However, this was due to the interpretation of entry into force of the TIEA with that partner (see Section C.1.9 *Be given effect through domestic law*). Further, the process of exchanging information related to criminal matters is the same as that for civil matters.

Provide information in specific form requested (ToR C.1.7)

344. There are no restrictions in Uruguay's exchange of information agreements that would prevent it from providing information in a specific form so long as this is consistent with its own administrative provisions. All of the seven new TIEAs concluded by Uruguay expressly allow for information to be provided in the specific form requested, to the extent allowable under the requested jurisdiction's domestic laws.

345. To date, Uruguay has not yet been requested to provide responses in a specific form to a treaty partner. However, in the event that information is requested in a specific form, officials from Uruguay's competent authority have reported that they will provide information in the specific form requested to the extent permitted under Uruguayan law and administrative practice.

In force (ToR C.1.8)

346. Exchange of information cannot take place unless a jurisdiction has exchange of information arrangements in force. Where exchange of information agreements have been signed, the international standard requires that jurisdictions must take all steps necessary to bring them into force expeditiously.

347. Uruguay presently has 31 EOI agreements to the standard, of which 22 agreements to the standard which are in force. The older agreement with Hungary does not include articles 26(4) and 26(5) but is interpreted by Uruguay consistently with the standard. Since 2011, Uruguay has ratified and brought into force two DTCs with Germany and Switzerland, signed in 2010. Internal procedures for ratification have been completed in Uruguay in relation to a further three DTCs, with Ecuador (signed 2011), Liechtenstein (signed 2010) and Portugal (signed 2009). DTCs signed with Finland, Korea, Malta and India, in Uruguay have entered into force.

348. In addition, Uruguay has also concluded 15 TIEAs, of which eight are currently in force. Uruguay should quickly take all steps necessary for its part, to bring all signed EOI agreements into force. Annex 3 sets out the dates of signature, and entry into force where relevant, of each of Uruguay's EOI agreements.

Signature and ratification in practice

349. In practice, requests to enter into an exchange of information agreement are usually received at the MEF or the Ministry of Foreign Affairs. The Department of Foreign Affairs will then proceed to acknowledge receipt and respond via the same channels with their own draft model agreement. Uruguay has never refused to enter into an exchange of information agreement. In order to strengthen its treaty network Uruguay has also been active in approaching treaty partners to negotiate an EOI agreement.

350. Once the Uruguayan authorities decide to negotiate with a particular jurisdiction, the body in charge of the negotiation is the tax advisory office at the Ministry, which is composed of 2 teams; one team in charge of negotiating DTC and the other one in charge of negotiating TIEAs.

351. When a request for a TIEA/DTC is received it will often be accompanied with the model TIEA of the requesting jurisdiction. The Uruguayan authorities then compare this model with their own template and the eventual agreement is negotiated; usually via electronic email correspondence for TIEAs but DTCs are always negotiated in person. Conference calls may also be used from time to time. It shall be noted that for TIEAs concluded with major trading partners (e.g. Brazil and Argentina), the TIEAs were negotiated in person. Officials from Uruguay have clarified that they always accept any request for a TIEA where it involves a "relevant partner" which means any country from which they receive a request to enter into a TIEA. To finalise the negotiation, the agreement is translated into Spanish in case it has been negotiated in another language and sent to the other contracting State for approval. Once the final text of the agreement has been agreed upon, the

agreement is sent to the office of the Chancellor (Ministry of Foreign Affairs) where they liaise with the office in the other jurisdiction for signature.

352. In accordance with the Constitution[38], upon signature the agreement will then be tabled in Parliament for ratification. The length of this process can vary depending on the jurisdiction, but the average ratification time out of 23 ratified agreements as of 15 July 2014 was 17.4 months. The ratification process is made through the passing of a law. Subsequently, the Minister of Finance conveys notice of ratification of exchange of information agreements via diplomatic channels to the treaty partner. On occasions where there have been some delays with bringing the agreement into force. However, delays were at times also attributable to the formalities of the other jurisdiction. The agreement is then published in the official Gazette, on the website of the Presidency of the Republic and on the DGI website. It is also added to the agreements listed in the DGI internal manual as used by all auditors.

353. One peer provided feedback that a TIEA signed on 14 December 2011 has not yet been ratified by Uruguay, such that the ratification process in this particular case exceeds 36 months. The Uruguayan authorities have written to that peer in May 2014 to inform them that they had ratified the agreement on 27 December 2012, and that such agreement entered into force on 7 January 2013.

354. Since 2009, Uruguay has made significant efforts to renegotiate agreements found not be to be to the standard and to negotiate new agreements in order to expand its EOI network. As at December 2014, Uruguay has completed negotiations for one TIEA and three DTCs. Negotiations are usually concluded over one or two rounds and on occasion three rounds of negotiation have been required. As at December 2014, there are 5 agreements (2 TIEAs and 3 DTCs) in various stages of negotiation.

Be given effect through domestic law (ToR C.1.9)

355. For information exchange to be effective the parties to an exchange of information arrangements need to enact any legislation necessary to comply with the terms of the arrangement. No specific legislation is required to bring the treaties into effect. Once ratified, treaties have the same effect as laws under the Uruguayan hierarchy of laws. The right of the Tax Administration Agency to access tax information to give effect to the EOI provisions in those agreements is found in Uruguayan domestic law, principally article 68 of the Tax Code. The Tax Reform Law 18 083 provides a specific exception to bank secrecy. Prior to 2012, Uruguay was unable to give full effect to its EOI agreements due to limitations in Uruguay's domestic law regarding access

38. Article 168 Num. 20 of the Constitution.

to information held by trustees (ToR C.1.3, C.1.4 and C.1.9). This limitation has now been removed by the article 19 of Law No. 18 930, which lifted the confidentiality obligation imposed on trustees by article 19 (c) of the Trusts Law, as described in Section B.1 of this report.

356. In practice two issues have arisen in relation to the application of the entry into force provisions in one of Uruguay's TIEAs, being the TIEA concluded between Uruguay and Argentina. This TIEA entered into force in February 2013, and constitutes a great improvement as no EOI mechanisms existed between the two jurisdictions prior to that period. The issues concern whether the treaty has retroactive effect for criminal tax matters and how it applies to information related to acts or facts predating the treaty but which are relevant for periods after the entry into force of the treaty. The two jurisdictions met twice in the first half of 2013 to establish general guidelines to complete the exchange of information effectively, but also to discuss the divergence of interpretation regarding the entry into force provision of the TIEA. No agreement was reached on the latter issue between the two jurisdictions.

The Criminal Tax Issue

357. All except one of the TIEAs concluded by Uruguay[39] provide for a distinction in the entry into force provisions between criminal tax matters and civil matters in the following terms:

> This Agreement shall enter into force on the date of the last notification, and shall thereupon have effect:
>
> (a) from [effective date] with respect to criminal tax matters; and
>
> (b) from [effective date] with respect to all other matters covered in Article 1 relating to taxable periods beginning on or after [effective date], or where there is no taxable period, all charges to tax arising on or after [effective date].

For all these TIEAs, Uruguay has confirmed that in respect to criminal tax matters, it would exchange information related to taxable period prior to the entry into force of the TIEAs.

358. With respect to the TIEA subject to a divergence of interpretation, however, the specific wording of the entry into force clause, set out below, differs somewhat from the others although the same distinction is made in respect of criminal and civil tax matters. Further the term "criminal tax matters" is also defined differently as "tax matters involving intentional acts *that*

39. This includes the TIEAs with Australia, Canada, Denmark, Faroe Islands, France, Greenland, Iceland,_the Netherlands, Sweden and the United Kingdom.

are subject to prosecution as stipulated by the criminal law of the requesting Party" [emphasis added][40]. Article 13(2) regarding the entry into force provides that:

> 2. *As from the date of its entry into force, this Agreement shall apply*:
>
> a) *In criminal tax matters on that date*, and; (emphasis added)
>
> b) In all other matters, on that date, but only for taxable periods beginning on or after that date or, where there is no taxable period, for tax collections arising on or after that date.

359. Argentina has argued that the entry into force provision in the TIEA obliges Uruguay to exchange information with respect to criminal tax matters in all cases, whether they relate to a taxable period after or before the entry into force of the TIEA, where Argentina had started prosecution in its own jurisdiction at the moment of making the request.

360. In contrast, the Uruguayan authorities have indicated that they understood during the negotiations with Argentina that it was agreed by the negotiators representing both parties that the TIEA would only apply to information generated after the entry into force of the TIEA. In addition, Uruguay stated that when the TIEA with Argentina was presented to the Uruguayan Parliament for approval, the Government explicitly indicated during the debates that the TIEA would not apply to information generated prior to the entry into force of the TIEA. Such interpretation was made public on more than one occasion in the parliamentary debates before the adoption of the TIEA. Nevertheless, the Uruguayan authorities have since refined their interpretation such that Uruguay will not provide information generated before the entry into force of the TIEA, whether in criminal or civil tax matters, if all the effects of that information were exhausted before the entry into force of the agreement (see paragraph 364 for further explanations).

361. Out of 14 income tax requests received from Argentina, eight requests dealt with criminal tax matters. Uruguay did not provide the information requested in any of the 8 cases on the grounds that the requested information pertained to taxable years prior to the entry into force of the agreement, as the audited period was between 2008 and 2012 in all cases (i.e. before the entry into force of the TIEA). It should be noted, however, that in these 8 cases, the taxpayers in question were subject to prosecution in the requesting jurisdiction at the time of making the EOI request to Uruguay. The peer presented the indictment for each of these cases which had been issued by the Court in March 2013 (i.e. after the entry into force of the TIEA).

---

40. Non-official translation from Spanish to English.

362. The international standard provides for exchange of past information which relates to a taxable period following the effective date, but the Terms of Reference do not require that information must be provided that relates to a taxable period before the entry into force of an information exchange agreement. Whether this is required in criminal tax matters will depend on the wording of the particular agreement. However, the wording of the entry into force provision of the TIEA which is subject to a divergence of interpretation does not differ in substance, apart from the definition of criminal tax matters, from other TIEAs concluded by Uruguay, which Uruguay interprets as allowing for retroactivity in criminal tax matters. It was therefore not possible to establish a more restrictive application than in Uruguay's other TIEAs with similar text. However, it is also acknowledged that this interpretative issue remains a bilateral matter with one jurisdiction.

The Issue of information relating to facts predating the TIEA

363. In addition, Argentina has indicated that requests aimed to establish tax obligations arising after the entry into force of the TIEA, were also declined on the ground that the information was generated prior to the entry into force of the agreement.

364. The Uruguayan authorities have indicated that its competent authority will exchange information produced before the entry into force of this agreement but relating to taxable periods after the entry into force of the agreement, both in criminal and civil tax matters under certain conditions. However, Uruguay does not provide information generated before the entry into force of the TIEA if all the effects of that information were exhausted before the entry into force of the agreement (e.g. invoices, information on shareholders which are no longer shareholders after the entry into force of the TIEA, information on companies liquidated prior to the entry into force of the TIEA). If, however, that past information still has effect after the entry into force – for example: bylaws of the company, contracts which helps determine the amortization for the taxable period after the entry into force – Uruguay will agree to exchange that information. Accordingly, for the application of this particular TIEA, a distinction is made by Uruguay between information which came into existence before the entry into force of the agreement but which has continuing effect and information which came into effect before the entry into force and which has no ongoing effect.

365. The Uruguayan authorities have clarified that the above-mentioned interpretation only applies to the TIEA concluded with Argentina. Out of 14 income tax received from that EOI partner, six requests related to civil tax matters, more specifically with withholding taxes. Uruguay provided the information in two cases and did not provide information in the four other cases. The refusal to provide the requested information in these four cases

was based on the fact that the information was generated – and its effects were exhausted – prior to the entry into force of the agreement. In all these cases, the invoices which constituted the information requested by the peer were issued prior to the entry into force of the agreement; i.e. in October 2012, December 2012 and January 2013.

366. Argentina confirmed that under its domestic law, the withholding tax is levied at the time of the payment to the non-resident recipient and that the payment date constitutes the taxable event, and hence the taxable period. In these four cases, the payment for the services rendered took place after the entry into force of the agreement (during the month of February 2013), such that the requested information was foreseeably relevant for the taxable period following the entry into force of the agreement. The requested information which was not provided by Uruguay consisted in copies of contracts of services, details concerning the services rendered, details of payments received/bank account, ownership information, bank transactions, and accounting records regarding the services rendered. In the two other cases, Uruguay provided the requested information as the payment related to the transactions invoiced was subject to withholding tax during the month of the entry into force of the TIEA; i.e. in February 2013. In these cases, the taxable period was also February 2013. Information requested by Argentina in situations where the above-mentioned bilateral interpretation did not arise was provided in all cases by Uruguay after the peer review period.

367. To conclude, the interpretation by Uruguay of this TIEA's entry into force provision is not in line with the standard, which provides for exchange of past information foreseeably relevant for a taxable period following the effective date of the agreement. As such, the criterion is not whether the information has continuing effect after the effective date, but rather whether the information is foreseeably relevant for the determination of the taxable period post effective date of the TIEA. This interpretation has prevented Uruguay to exchange information in four EOI civil tax cases. Uruguay should ensure that the interpretation of its TIEA with that peer does not restrict the exchange of information generated prior to the entry into force of the TIEA but relevant for the assessment of tax years beginning after the entry into force of the TIEAs.

Determination and factors underlying recommendations

Phase 1 determination	
The element is in place.	
Factors underlying recommendations	**Recommendations**
Uruguay has signed two TIEAs in 2012 which it has not yet taken all steps necessary, for its part, to bring into force.	Uruguay should take all steps necessary for its part, to bring each of its signed EOI agreements into force as quickly as possible.

Phase 2 Rating	
Largely Compliant	
Factors underlying recommendations	**Recommendations**
The interpretation by Uruguay of the entry into force provision of one TIEA concluded with a significant EOI partner during the peer review period is not in line with the international standard.	Uruguay must ensure that its interpretation of the entry into force provision of that TIEA does not restrict the exchange of information with that EOI partner.

C.2. Exchange of information mechanisms with all relevant partners

The jurisdictions' network of information exchange mechanisms should cover all relevant partners.

368. Ultimately, the international standard requires that jurisdictions exchange information with all relevant partners, meaning those partners who are interested in entering into an information exchange arrangement. Agreements cannot be concluded only with counterparties without economic significance. If it appears that a jurisdiction is refusing to enter into agreements or negotiations with partners, in particular ones that have a reasonable expectation of requiring information from that jurisdiction in order to properly administer and enforce its tax laws; it may indicate a lack of commitment to implement the standards.

369. Uruguay signed its first DTC with Germany in 1987 followed by a DTC with Hungary in 1988. In 2009, it commenced a programme of expanding its EOI network, signing double tax conventions with Mexico, Spain and Portugal in 2009; with Switzerland and Liechtenstein, as well as an update to its DTC with Germany and a TIEA with France in 2010, and a DTC with Ecuador, Finland, India, Korea and Malta in 2011. In 2012, it concluded a DTC with Romania, and a TIEA with Argentina, Australia, Brazil, and the

Netherlands. In 2013, it concluded a TIEA with the Canada, United-Kingdom and a DTC with Viet Nam and Belgium. It has now signed a total 31 EOI agreements, which are to the standard, 22 of which are currently in force.

370. Uruguay is a signatory to the Mercosur San Luis Treaty 1996 (with Argentina, Brazil, and Paraguay), which entered into force in 2001, but this agreement does not cover mutual legal assistance for criminal tax matters.

371. As noted in the introduction to the report Uruguay's main trade partners are Brazil, and Argentina, and to a lesser extent, China, the US and Mexico. Uruguay has expanded its EOI network by concluding in total 27 EOI agreements since 2009, 15 of which are currently in force. Of note, Uruguay concluded a TIEA with two of its trading partners, being Argentina and Brazil. The TIEA with Argentina entered into force on 7 February 2013, while the TIEA with Brazil, signed on 24 October 2012, is pending ratification, both from Uruguay and Brazil's side. This development is reflected in Annex 2 of this report. Uruguay continues to expand its EOI network. Uruguay has or is currently negotiating TIEAs with two jurisdictions and DTCs with three jurisdictions. In summary, Uruguay's network of information exchange agreements covers all relevant partners.

Determination and factors underlying recommendations

Phase 1 determination	
The element is in place.	
Factors underlying recommendations	**Recommendations**
	Uruguay should continue to develop and rapidly expand its network of EOI arrangements with all relevant partners, and take all steps necessary to bring concluded agreements into effect as quickly as possible.

Phase 2 Rating
Compliant

C.3. Confidentiality

> The jurisdictions' mechanisms for exchange of information should have adequate provisions to ensure the confidentiality of information received.

Information received: disclosure, use, and safeguards (ToR C.3.1)

372. Governments would not engage in information exchange without the assurance that the information provided would only be used for the purposes permitted under the exchange mechanisms and that its confidentiality would be preserved. Information exchange instruments must therefore contain confidentiality provisions that spell out specifically to whom the information can be disclosed and the purposes for which the information can be used. In addition to the protections afforded by the confidentiality of EOI arrangements, countries with tax systems generally impose strict confidentiality requirements on information collected for tax purposes. Confidentiality rules should apply to all types of information exchanged, including information provided in a request, information transmitted in response to a request and any background documents to such requests.

373. Each of the EOI agreements concluded by Uruguay meet the standard for confidentiality reflected in Article 26(2) of the OECD Model Taxation Convention and Article 8 of the OECD Model TIEA respectively.

374. These confidentiality requirements are supported by Uruguay's domestic law which includes significant sanctions for breach. Article 47 of the Tax Code requires the DGI and its officers to keep all information which they have as a result of their administrative or judicial functions confidential, and it shall only be disclosed when it is essential for the due performance of their functions and based on a well-founded request. Failure to comply will be cause for dismissal from employment for the officer.

375. However, Uruguay's special regime for accessing bank information may not be consistent with the confidentiality provisions of its EOI agreements in all instances. The judicial process for accessing bank information requires the disclosure of certain information to the court, and also the relevant account-holder. Whilst disclosure to the taxpayer of information concerning an EOI request is foreseen by the international standard, the account holder will not in all cases be the taxpayer (or their proxy). In those cases, the release of information to that person is inconsistent with the standard.

376. Although the special regime for accessing bank information has not been tested in practice during the peer review period, the Uruguayan competent authorities have clarified that the joint team created with attorneys to deal with cases where banking information has been requested and to prepare special guidelines for the collaboration with judges, would adhere to strict

confidentiality rules. In addition, Uruguay has confirmed that in the notice letter for voluntary disclosure, no information regarding the EOI request is disclosed to the account holder (in particular, the name of the requesting jurisdiction is not mentioned). It shall be noted that this procedure applies both for domestic tax purposes and for EOI purposes, and the notice only indicates the bank information needed. The EOI request may on occasion need to be disclosed to the judge upon his request, but would not be disclosed to the taxpayer.

All other information exchanged (ToR C.3.2)

377. The confidentiality provisions in Uruguay's domestic law, notably Article 47 of the Tax Code, applies equally to protect the request for information itself and includes background documents provided by an applicant State, as well as any other information relating to the request such as communications between the EOI partners in respect of the requests. The issue of disclosure of information to a person who is not the taxpayer, in the course of court proceedings to access bank information which is described in section B.1.5 of the report, applies to all the information exchanged in the course of an EOI requested.

Confidentiality in practice

378. Uruguay has strict processes and procedures in place to ensure confidentiality of taxpayer information both for domestic and EOI purposes. Two resolutions – Resolution No. 1176/2013, dated April 18 2013 and Resolution No. 1176/2013 – guarantee the confidentiality of the information.

Human resources

379. Prior to any formal appointment with the DGI, all candidates are required to undergo comprehensive background and security checks to ensure that they will not pose any risk to security. Once appointed, all employees are subject to confidentiality obligations as set out in the terms of their employment. All confidentiality obligations, processes and procedures are clearly outlined and explained during the induction training that all employees must undertake at the commencement of their employment with the DGI. Internal training is also systematically provided to remind and update employees on their confidentiality obligations and procedures.

380. Resolution No. 1176/2013 establishes that the Head of the DGI is in charge of supervising and assessing the confidentiality of all proceedings, suggesting any necessary adjustments, and that "all employees involved in managing the EOI – whatever the nature of their relationship with the Tax

Authority – are subject to the strictest confidentiality rules, and if they failed to comply they would be subject to the corresponding criminal, administrative, and civil liabilities".

381. Resolution No. 1177/2013, dated April 18, 2013, which includes a chapter with guidelines on confidentiality, makes reference to the above-mentioned measures and establishes that "all employees involved in this procedure – whatever the nature of their relationship with the Tax Authority are subject to the strictest confidentiality rules, and if they failed to comply they would be subject to the corresponding criminal, administrative, and civil liabilities". This applies to people who are no longer public servants or people working for the Administration under contract.

Facilities

382. Physical security for the confidentiality of all information/documents and computer equipment belonging to the EOI Unit is also strictly maintained. The EOI Unit is located within the DGI building, and the public are not authorised to enter the DGI building except for limited areas, accompanied at all times by DGI officials. All visitors must register at the front desk security. The DGI building has 24 hour security guards on duty.

Storage and processing of incoming requests

383. All EOI requests are made or received through the competent authority, being the head of the Large Taxpayers Division of the International Taxation Department (ITD). In practice, EOI requests are received via courier, registered or regular mail where they are immediately forwarded to the ITD. A hard file is opened for each request and kept in a secure cabinet within the ITD which is locked with a key at all times. It is the policy of ITD that only two members of staff have access to this cabinet; being the person responsible for EOI and the head of the Large Taxpayer Division.

384. Each employee has a unique user ID and password and cannot access their PC without the use of a password that must be used at all times in order to access their PCs. These measures ensure that access to highly confidential information such as EOI requests is limited. The DGI also has many internal measures in place to ensure that confidentiality practices are being respected by all employees concerned with the EOI process. All information or printed files that are not meant to be kept shall be destroyed using shredders.

385. In the course of accessing the requested information, internal email exchanges within the DGI can be sent via secure encrypted email in case the requests are of sensitive nature or where extra confidentiality measures are required. All internal and external communications must be done with sealed

envelopes with the administrative file number, the country requesting the information, and the reference number written in front, and the words "confidential" and "urgent" written across the envelopes. All necessary measures must be taken to guarantee the recipient receives the envelope in person. Whenever a document is to be sent to another person, division or unit within the organisation, a receipt must be signed by its addressee/receiver, confirming the document is under his custody. Documents are kept in restricted access locations.

386. Once an exchange of information process is completed, all supporting data is placed in a closed envelope with the administrative file number written in front. On providing the information to the treaty partner, materials are always sent via registered mail, whereby a mail tracking function is in place. A copy of any documents requested is kept at the ITD office which is separate from the general file location of the DGI, whilst a copy of the request and the cover letter is maintained for reference purposes at the offices of the competent authority.

Enforcement and penalties

387. If there is an unauthorised disclosure of information related to an international exchange of information, an administrative investigation must be ordered (Article 180 of Decree No. 500/991) and at the same time reported to the Director General's Office, regardless of the obligation to report its results once it is completed. In such a case, the final report shall include in all cases recommendations to minimise the incident's consequences, an analysis of what must be done in the future to avoid similar incidents, and recommendations to take actions or apply sanctions against the people allegedly responsible for the violation, pointing out that law enforcement authorities may act if premeditated disclosure is suspected. In addition, the legal department has issued an internal memorandum which concluded that ex-employees of the DGI remain liable for any breach of confidentiality regarding matters covered by their former employment with the DGI.

388. Feedback from peers indicates that there have been no issues with confidentiality as it relates to exchange of information requests to date. The Uruguayan authorities have confirmed that, there have been no cases in which information received by the competent authority from an EOI partner has been made public or disclosed to a third party other than in accordance with the terms under which it was provided and the international standard.

Determination and factors underlying recommendations

Phase 1 determination
The element is in place.

Phase 2 Rating
Compliant

C.4. Rights and safeguards of taxpayers and third parties

The exchange of information mechanisms should respect the rights and safeguards of taxpayers and third parties.

Exceptions to requirement to provide information (ToR C.4.1)

389. The international standard permits requested parties to not supply information in response to a request in certain identified situations. Among other reasons, information is not required to be provided where it would disclose confidential communications protected by the attorney-client privilege. Attorney-client privilege is a feature of the legal systems of many countries. However, communications between a client and an attorney or another admitted legal representative are, generally, only privileged to the extent that the attorney or other legal representative acts in his or her capacity as an attorney or legal representative. Where attorney-client privilege is more broadly defined, it does not provide valid grounds on which information can be declined to be provided in response to a request.

390. Each of Uruguay's EOI agreements includes provisions allowing for the requesting jurisdiction to decline to provide information which would disclose any trade, business, industrial, commercial or professional secrets (which would include legal privilege). They also provide discretion on disclosing information which would be contrary to public policy. These provisions are consistent with Article 26(3)(c) of the OECD Model Tax Convention and Article 7(3) of the Model TIEA.

391. Article 302 of the Criminal Code states that: "Persons who, without fair cause, reveal secrets that would come to their knowledge, by virtue of their profession, employment or representation, shall be punished by a fine of one hundred to six hundred units indexed, if the act causes harm" (emphasis added). As set out in Annex 1 to the Phase 1 Report, Uruguay has clarified that "[t]he violation of professional secrecy is a crime stated in article 302 Criminal Code, this article allows the professional to plead "fair cause" and to give the information required. Besides, he can also plead the "complying with the law" grounds set out in article 28, Criminal Code as an exemption:

in this case, the obligation to comply with article 68 and 70 of the Tax Code. This last article states the obligation to comply with the [Tax Administration Authority]."

392. Since 2012, Law No. 18 930 expressly lifted *(i)* the secrecy obligation imposed on trustees by Article 19(c) of the Trusts Law when information is sought by the DGI or the BCU (article 19); and *(ii)* the professional secrecy provisions established by the Stock Market Act and the Investment Funds Act when ownership information regarding bearer shares and foreign companies is sought by the DGI (article 21). Therefore, Law No. 18 930 narrowed down the uncertainty concerning the scope of professional secrecy under Uruguayan law.

393. Uruguay has also provided some decisions from judicial and administrative concerning the interpretation of professional secrecy provisions with respect to information held by legal professionals. The decisions demonstrate that professional secrecy cannot be claimed by an attorney as a valid defence against the disclosure of information to authorities in order to conceal either a criminal or unlawful act of the attorney himself/herself or by another person. Uruguay has also clarified that, other than the material already provided, Uruguayan authorities could not find court decisions dealing with the interaction of Article 302 of the Criminal Code (reproduced above) and the tax authorities access powers established under the Tax Code.

394. Given the legislative changes introduced by Law No. 18 930 and further court decisions, a potential gap concerning the scope of the professional secrecy exception established by Article 302 of the Criminal Code is likely to be narrow. Operation of attorney-client privilege in practice.

395. In practice, the Uruguayan authorities have confirmed that, for domestic tax purposes, the professional secrecy exception in relation to lawyers is interpreted and applied in a restrictive manner which does not prevent tax authorities from accessing books of account, working papers and other documentation held by lawyers where they exercise their information gathering powers. In relation to domestic tax issues, the Uruguayan officials have confirmed that claims of attorney-client privilege have never arisen in practice.

396. From those peers that provided peer input, none indicated that professional secrecy has ever caused any issues in practice in relation to EOI. There have been no cases in which an EOI request has been denied or in which, as a result of the information provided, an entity or individual has raised an objection founded on professional secrecy. Officials from the DGI have advised that in the event that they were to receive a claim of attorney-client privilege over information requested pursuant to an EOI request, the above exception of complying with the law (in this case EOI tax laws) set out in article 28 of

the Criminal Code would be used to clearly override this claim. Therefore, the scope of attorney-client privilege is quite narrow in scope and should not affect the effective exchange of information in practice.

Determination and factors underlying recommendations

Phase 1 determination
The element is in place.

Phase 2 Rating
Compliant

C.5. Timeliness of responses to requests for information

> The jurisdiction should provide information under its network of agreements in a timely manner.

Responses within 90 days (ToR C.5.1)

397. In order for exchange of information to be effective it needs to be provided in a timeframe which allows tax authorities to apply the information to the relevant cases. If a response is provided but only after a significant lapse of time the information may no longer be of use to the requesting authorities. This is particularly important in the context of international co-operation as cases in this area must be of sufficient important to warrant making a request.

398. With respect to information protected by bank secrecy, Uruguay has in place a court-based system to lift the application of bank secrecy where the information is sought for EOI purposes, in case the bank account holder does not voluntary authorise the lifting of bank secrecy according to the procedure set out in section B.1.5 *Secrecy provisions*. Uruguay has advised that at most, this process could take up to 180 days to be completed.

399. It is also noted that in the protocol to the Uruguay – Ecuador DTC and in the protocol to the Uruguay-Spain DTC, a requested party is only required to provide the information within 180 days. In the event the information cannot be provided within that time, the requested jurisdiction is to indicate the reason for the delay. No reference is made to providing a status update to the requesting party. However, none of the above-mentioned provisions would prevent Uruguay from providing an update on the status of the request to the EOI partner within 90 days.

Timeliness in practice

400. Uruguay received 17 direct tax requests from 4 jurisdictions, 14 of which were made from one of Uruguay's main trading partners over the review period. Out of the 17 requests, five were considered valid requests and responded to by the Uruguayan competent authority. All the requested information was provided in four cases, but one of these requests was withdrawn from the treaty partner (see Section B.2. *Notification requirements and Rights and Safeguards*). There were two requests received in 2011, one received in 2012 and 22 requests received in 2013 (until 30 June 2013).

	July 2010-June 2011		July 2011-June 2012		July 2012-June 2013		Total	
	num.	%	num.	%	num.	%	Num.	%
Total number of direct tax requests received	-	-	2	100	14*	100	16*	100
Full response: ≤90 days			1		0		1	6.25**
≤180 days (cumulative)			-	-	0		2	12.5**
≤1 year (cumulative)			-	-	-	-	-	-
>1 year			1		-	-	1	6.25**
Declined due to the interpretation by Uruguay of the entry into force provision of the TIEA signed with Argentina					12		12	75**
Failure to obtain and provide information requested			0		0		0	
Requests still pending at date of review			0		0		0	

* Originally, Uruguay received 17 direct tax requests, but one was withdrawn in 2012 by the treaty partner.

** If the requests declined due to the interpretation by Uruguay of the entry into force provision of the TIEA signed with Argentina are excluded from the computation, Uruguay was able to answer within 90 days in 25% of the cases, within 180 days in 50% of the case and in 25% of the cases after one year.

401. Uruguayan officials have confirmed that any requests regarding a person in which more than one piece of information is requested are still considered to be a single request. However, in cases where information is requested about several people, a file is created for each of them and the number of requests is equivalent to the number of people about whom information has been requested. A further request for information on the same matter where the original request has not yet been fully satisfied would be considered to be a new request according to the contents of the requesting State's new request and it would be responded making reference to the original request.

402. Officials have confirmed that the time period commences on the date that they receive the request. Due to interpretation issues concerning one of its EOI agreements, information was not provided in all cases (see s. C.1.9 for more details). However where a request was not answered the reason for this decision was provided in all cases. For of the 17 income tax request received, the average time to respond to a request was 89 days (including those requests in which they could not provide the information). Excluding those requests in which they did not provide the information, the average response time was 189 days. However, this average may not be very representative of the practice of Uruguay, as the sample represents only five requests in direct income taxes (which includes one request withdrawn). Except for the specific case mentioned below for which the response to the peer took more than a year, peers were generally satisfied with the timeliness of response of Uruguay.

403. Officials from the ITD have made clarifications to the requesting jurisdiction in eight cases over the review period. In cases where clarifications were made officials have confirmed that they do not exclude the time taken by the requesting jurisdiction to respond to their request for clarification. In six of these cases, the request for clarification aim to clarify the transactions subject to the requests, whereas in two other cases, an element of the request (i.e. an authentication) was missing.

404. There was one specific case during the review period for which Uruguay took over one year to respond. The request was first received in August 2011 when Uruguay was in the process of setting up its EOI operations (in September 2011 Decree 313/2011 came into force formally delegating the power to the DGI to act as competent authority for EOI purposes and Decree 337/2011 created the ITD and the EOI Unit). Although in force since 1994, the exchange of information article in the DTC had never been used. Uruguay responded by notifying the Ministry of Economy of the requesting jurisdiction and also the person who signed the request of the identity of the Uruguayan competent authority and requested confirmation of the name of the competent authority in in the requesting jurisdiction. No response was received. The case was only progressed when the Uruguayan competent authority met in person with the competent authority from the requesting jurisdiction on the fringes of an OECD competent authority meeting in May 2012. Overall, the process of verification of the competent authority of the requesting jurisdiction took seven months and this delayed the provision of information in practice. At the time of receipt of the request, Uruguay had not yet established its competent authority database. Officials in Uruguay have confirmed that they now use the competent authority database to verify the competent authority details and if the signatory of the request is different they then send an email to verify the identity of the competent authority. As a result no such delay has since occurred.

405. In the case where information could not be provided within 90 days, officials from the EOI Unit did not regularly send status updates to the requesting jurisdiction. However, a procedure has since been put in place to ensure that regular status updates will now be sent for all future requests. Over the review period all requests were recorded in an excel spreadsheet. In addition, the Uruguayan authorities have confirmed that since early 2014, they have started submitting partial responses as the requested information becomes available, including an update on the status of the remaining information.

Organisational process and resources *(ToR C.5.2)*

Organisational process

406. Prior to September 2011[41], exchange of information operated on an ad-hoc basis in Uruguay. However, since that time, a formal EOI Unit has been implemented with set processes for all aspects related to EOI. For EOI purposes in Uruguay the Minister for Finance is the competent authority and he has delegated this authority to the DGI. Internally within the DGI this power has been delegated via internal resolution to the Deputy Director, the head of the Large Taxpayer Division and the head of the International Tax Department (ITD). The ITD is responsible for the day to day processing of EOI requests.

Handling of EOI requests

407. Generally, EOI requests are received at the office of the Director-General of the DGI. Each time an EOI agreement comes into force, the DGI makes contact with the EOI partner to clarify the competent authority for EOI purposes in the requesting jurisdiction. There is an annual allocated budget for EOI purposes each year within the DGI (for mailing costs, etc.)

408. When a request for information is received at the office of the DGI, an immediate acknowledgement of receipt is sent via email to the requesting jurisdiction. A file is opened for EOI purposes at the office of the Director-General which is given a different cover, and the EOI request is then placed within an envelope inside this file. A confidentiality stamp is also on the cover of the file. It is then sent to the Large Taxpayer Division, which in turn, reviews the request and sends it to the ITD who will carry out the day-to-day operations in relation to EOI matters.

409. Once the EOI Unit has performed a preliminary assessment of the request (these steps are documented under steps A1 – A3 in the EOI Manual)

41. The International Tax Department (ITD) and EOI Unit was established on September 22, 2011 by way of Decree N° 337/2011.

and determines the request to be valid and in line with the terms of the EOI agreement, the EOI officer then makes an assessment of the information to be collected. Officials from the EOI Unit have confirmed that they abide by the "four eye" principle of review whereby an analyst from the ITD will confer with the director of the ITD.

410. When a request arrives at the office of the ITD, a hard copy is filed and the request is stored within a safe deposit box within the ITD. Only officials within the ITD have access to this safe deposit box. Officials from Uruguay have confirmed that they implement clean desk principles and all files are always stored within the safe deposit box. The only persons with keys to the safety deposit box are the head of the ITD and the head of the large taxpayer unit. Security cameras have also been installed and there is a dedicated office shredder utilised only for EOI purposes.

411. Once the request has been determined as valid, the EOI Unit assesses to see if the information is available in the databases accessible to the DGI (see s. B.1 for more information). In cases where information is available within the DGI, but within another department such as the National Internal Audit, ITD prepares an internal memo setting out the requested information. This internal memo is subject to the same confidentiality characteristics and is sent internally via sealed envelope. The department, from which the information has been requested, is given a timeframe as determined by the head of the ITD and the head of the Large Taxpayer Division. Generally, the timeframe given is a period of five days.

412. In those cases where the information is not available within the DGI, the ITD may determine the information to be accessible in another government database and in those cases, similar to when information in requested within the DGI, a memo is drafted and a time period of five days is generally given in which to produce the information. And in all cases over the review period information has been produced both by other departments within the DGI and other government organisations within the five day working period.

413. Where the information has to be accessed from a third party, a letter detailing the required information is prepared. This summons letter will usually be dispatched by an official from the ITD who is processing the request and who may be accompanied by another official from the ITD. The summons letter may also be delivered by members from the large taxpayer unit or by a team as appointed by resolution from the DGI. The team who will deliver this summons will depend on the size of the taxpayer. The summons letter is always hand-delivered to the third party in order to access the information. Generally, the information is requested to be provided on the spot. In the case that the information cannot be provided on the spot, a summons is issued to the third person to appear in person at the offices of the DGI to produce the information within 48 hours.

414. Once the request has been satisfied and the information has been provided to the ITD, the EOI official prepares a summary of the request and a letter is prepared setting out the requested information. The letter is reviewed by the head of the ITD. Once the letter has been finalised, the letter is sent to the office of the large taxpayer unit who then dispatches the letter to the office of the Director-General who will then sign the letter. Once signed, the letter is sent to the large taxpayer unit where it is dispatched by the ITD to the requesting jurisdiction.

415. The letter setting out the information and any accompanying documents (the originals) are placed in a sealed envelope and dispatched to the requesting jurisdiction via courier. A receipt of postage is maintained by the EOI Unit and placed on the hard copy file dedicated to the request. Certified copies of all original documents are maintained indefinitely on the file and the originals are returned to the owner. Uruguay has confirmed that they track the sent information until such time they see that it has been successfully received by the requesting jurisdiction. Officials from the EOI Unit have reported that they seek feedback from treaty partners when they dispatch an EOI request and they have received this in very few cases.

416. As outlined above, Uruguay's competent authority has experienced difficulties in processing certain requests due to treaty interpretation issues (see section C.1.9).

Resources

417. Prior to September 2011, there was no formal EOI Unit in Uruguay and EOI was conducted on an ad-hoc basis. Decree 337/011 created the International Tax Department (ITD) which is the body responsible for the day to day processing of EOI requests, amongst other activities. There are seven permanent officials within the ITD including five accountants and two lawyers. All seven officials have been trained in EOI both internally and have also attended Global Forum "The Last Mile" training and are actively involved in the processing of EOI requests. All staff is regularly reminded of their confidentiality obligations both for domestic and EOI purposes. On a wider level, the DGI has also conducted internal EOI sensitisation training for over 200 auditors within the DGI. Officials from Uruguay have indicated that they are well staffed for EOI purposes.

418. The competent authority uses the following performance measures or indicators to monitor the EOI management:

- Compliance with the deadlines set forth in the Procedure;
- Number of processed requests for information (total, by year, by country, and by year and by country); and

- Response time for received requests (total, by year, by country, and by year and by country).

419. Two reports are prepared by the ITD: one detailing "responses" only as final responses, and another interpreting" responses" as both final and partial responses (if any). The results of these measures or indicators have an impact on the assessment and grading of the employees that participate in the management of the EOI.

420. The Uruguayan authorities have clarified that they will put in place a computer application to manage requests for the international EOI based on DGI Resolution No 4502/2013, which is operational since 1 January 2015. This application consist in a management system for EOI upon request, which will have a deadline control system and will also control the procedure and the stages the requests are in, in order complete EOI efficiently.

Absence of restrictive conditions on exchange of information (ToR C.5.3)

421. Exchange of information assistance should not be subject to unreasonable, disproportionate, or unduly restrictive conditions. Other than those matters identified earlier in this report, there are no other unreasonable, disproportionate or unduly restrictive conditions on exchange of information existing in practice.

Conclusion

422. The procedures established by the DGI, which are included in an EOI Manual, appear to be sufficient to handle incoming requests in a timely manner. The resources currently allocated to the DGI appear sufficient to deal with the present workload. However, due to the reasons set out in Section C.1, out of 17 requests, Uruguay provided information in only 5 income tax cases during the three-year period under review. Consequently, the organisational processes have not been sufficiently tested in practice. Accordingly, it is recommended that Uruguay keeps monitoring the practical implementation of the organisational processes of the competent authority. The monitoring should also cover the level of resources committed to EOI purposes, especially in the event of a significant increase in the number of incoming EOI requests.

Determination and factors underlying recommendations

Phase 1 determination
This element involves issues of practice that are assessed in the Phase 2 review. Accordingly no Phase 1 determination has been made.

Phase 2 rating	
Largely compliant	
Factors underlying recommendation	**Recommendation**
Uruguay has resources and organisational processes in place that appear to be adequate for dealing with incoming EOI requests. However, out of 17 requests received over the review period, Uruguay processed only five EOI income tax requests during the three-year period under review due to the reasons set out in Section C.1.9. Consequently, the organisational processes for EOI have not been sufficiently tested in practice.	Uruguay should continue to monitor the practical implementation of the organisational processes of the competent authority as well as the level of resources committed to EOI purposes, in particular taking account of any significant changes to the volume of incoming EOI requests, to ensure that both the processes and level of resources are adequate for effective EOI in practice.
Uruguay did not provide an update or status report to its EOI partners within 90 days when the competent authority was not able to provide a substantive response within that time, unless it was specifically requested by the treaty partner.	Uruguay should ensure that updates to EOI partners are provided within 90 days in those cases where it is not possible to provide a partial or complete response within that timeframe.

Summary of Determinations and Factors Underlying Recommendations

Overall Rating
Largely compliant

Determination	Factors underlying recommendations	Recommendations
Jurisdictions should ensure that ownership and identity information for all relevant entities and arrangements is available to their competent authorities *(ToR A.1.)*		
Phase 1 determination: The element is in place.		
Phase 2 rating: Largely Compliant	Legal requirements have been introduced for the reporting of ownership information in relation to bearer shares in all cases. However, some of these legal requirements such as the extinction of shareholder rights for non-reporting and the mandatory liquidation of non-compliant bearer share companies, have only recently come into force and their effectiveness could not be assessed in practice by the assessment team.	Uruguay should continue to monitor the mandatory liquidation of non-compliant bearer share companies and ensure that information on the owners of bearer shares is made fully available in all cases.
Jurisdictions should ensure that reliable accounting records are kept for all relevant entities and arrangements *(ToR A.2.)*		
Phase 1 determination: The element is in place.		

Determination	Factors underlying recommendations	Recommendations
Phase 2 rating: Largely Compliant	Experience with the record keeping requirements in respect of underlying accounting documentation and the filing requirements of annual accounts, which applies to entities not subject to tax since August 2012, is limited.	Uruguay should ensure that its monitoring and enforcement powers are sufficiently exercised in practice to support the record keeping and filing requirements applicable to entities not subject to tax in Uruguay
Banking information should be available for all account-holders *(ToR A.3.)*		
Phase 1 determination: The element is in place.		
Phase 2 rating: Compliant		
Competent authorities should have the power to obtain and provide information that is the subject of a request under an exchange of information arrangement from any person within their territorial jurisdiction who is in possession or control of such information (irrespective of any legal obligation on such person to maintain the secrecy of the information) *(ToR B.1.)*		
Phase 1 determination: The element is in place, but certain aspects of the legal implementation of the element need improvement.	Uruguay's ability to access bank information prior to 2 January 2011 is limited under its domestic legislation.	Uruguay should ensure that all relevant bank information may be accessed for EOI purposes, regardless of the period to which the information relates, to ensure they can give full effect to their EOI agreements.
Phase 2 rating: Partially Compliant	During the peer review period, Uruguay did not gather banking information from banks concerning information on transactions taking place before 2 January 2011 for exchange of information purposes. In addition, Uruguay did not gather banking information from banks concerning information on transactions taking place after 2 January 2011, although it has done so after the peer review period. Accordingly, the effectiveness of the access powers could not be assessed.	Uruguay should ensure that all relevant bank information may be accessed for exchange of information purposes and monitor the implementation of the access powers in practice.

Determination	Factors underlying recommendations	Recommendations
The rights and safeguards (e.g. notification, appeal rights) that apply to persons in the requested jurisdiction should be compatible with effective exchange of information *(ToR B.2.)*		
Phase 1 determination: The element is in place, but certain aspects of the legal implementation of the element need improvement.	Under the court process for accessing bank information, certain information must be provided to the Uruguayan court to which the relevant account-holder (often the taxpayer) will have access. There are no exceptions to this notification of the account-holder prior to exchange of information, for example for cases where the information requested is of a very urgent nature, or where prior notification is likely to undermine the chance of success of the investigation in the requesting jurisdiction.	Uruguay should ensure that disclosure of information relating to an EOI request in the course of the court process to access bank information includes appropriate exceptions to notification prior to exchange of the information.
	Decree no. 313/011, as amended, requires the prior notification of the individual or the entity concerned prior to the tax authority's decision on responding to an incoming EOI request. It is not clear that there are appropriate exceptions from this prior notification procedure.	It is recommended that Uruguay clarifies that suitable exceptions from prior notification requirement are permitted to facilitate effective exchange of information (e.g. in cases in which the information requested is of a very urgent nature or the notification is likely to undermine the chance of the success of the investigation conducted by the requesting jurisdiction).
Phase 2 rating: Partially Compliant		

Determination	Factors underlying recommendations	Recommendations
Exchange of information mechanisms should allow for effective exchange of information *(ToR C.1.)*		
Phase 1 determination: The element is in place.	Uruguay has signed two TIEAs (in 2012 which it has not yet taken all steps necessary, for its part, to bring into force.	Uruguay should take all steps necessary for its part, to bring each of its signed EOI agreements into force as quickly as possible.
Phase 2 rating: Largely Compliant	The interpretation by Uruguay of the entry into force provision of one TIEA concluded with a significant EOI partner during the peer review period is not in line with the international standard.	Uruguay must ensure that its interpretation of the entry into force provision of that TIEA does not restrict the exchange of information with that EOI partner.
The jurisdictions' network of information exchange mechanisms should cover all relevant partners *(ToR C.2.)*		
Phase 1 determination: The element is in place.		Uruguay should continue to develop and rapidly expand its network of EOI arrangements with all relevant partners, and take all steps necessary to bring concluded agreements into effect as quickly as possible.
Phase 2 rating: Compliant		
The jurisdictions' mechanisms for exchange of information should have adequate provisions to ensure the confidentiality of information received *(ToR C.3.)*		
Phase 1 determination: The element is in place.		
Phase 2 rating: Compliant		
The exchange of information mechanisms should respect the rights and safeguards of taxpayers and third parties *(ToR C.4.)*		
Phase 1 determination: The element is in place.		
Phase 2 rating: Compliant		

Determination	Factors underlying recommendations	Recommendations
The jurisdiction should provide information under its network of agreements in a timely manner *(ToR C.5.)*		
Phase 1 determination: This element involves issues of practice that are assessed in the Phase 2 review. Accordingly no Phase 1 determination has been made.		
Phase 2 rating: Largely Compliant	Uruguay has resources and organisational processes in place that appear to be adequate for dealing with incoming EOI requests. However, out of 17 requests received over the review period, Uruguay processed only five EOI income tax requests during the three-year period under review due to the reasons set out in section C.1.9. Consequently, the organisational processes for EOI have not been sufficiently tested in practice.	Uruguay should continue to monitor the practical implementation of the organisational processes of the competent authority as well as the level of resources committed to EOI purposes, in particular taking account of any significant changes to the volume of incoming EOI requests, to ensure that both the processes and level of resources are adequate for effective EOI in practice.
	Uruguay did not provide an update or status report to its EOI partners within 90 days when the competent authority was not able to provide a substantive response within that time, unless it was specifically requested by the treaty partner.	Uruguay should ensure that updates to EOI partners are provided within 90 days in those cases where it is not possible to provide a partial or complete response within that timeframe.

Annex 1: Jurisdiction's response to the review report[42]

Uruguay wishes to acknowledge the hard work involved to produce this Phase 2 Report, which reasonably reflects the situation of our country in terms of transparency and exchange of information for tax purposes.

42. This Annex presents the jurisdiction's response to the review report and shall not be deemed to represent the Global Forum's views.

Annex 2: List of all exchange of information mechanisms

Bilateral agreements

The table below contains the list of information exchange agreements (TIEA) and tax treaties (DTC) signed by Uruguay as of December 2014.

Jurisdiction	Type of EoI arrangement	Date signed	Date entered into force/status
Argentina	TIEA	23 Apr 2012	7 Feb 2013
Australia	TIEA	10 Dec 2012	1 July 2014
Belgium	DTC	23 Aug 2013	
Brazil	TIEA	23 Oct 2012	Not in force. Ratified by Uruguay on 29 Dec 2014
Canada	TIEA	05 Feb 2013	27 Jun 2014
Chile	TIEA	12 Sep 2014	
Denmark	TIEA	14 Dec 2011	7 Jan 2013
Ecuador	DTC	26 May 2011	15 Nov 2011
Faroe Islands	TIEA	14 Dec 2011	Not in force. Ratified by Uruguay on 27 Dec 2012
Finland	DTC	13 Dec 2011	6 Feb 2013
France	TIEA	28 Jan 2010	31 Dec 2010
Germany	DTC	5 May 1987	1 Jan 1991
		9 Mar 2010	1 Jan 2012
Greenland	TIEA	14 Dec 2011	25 Jan 2013
Guernsey	TIEA	2 Jul 2014	
Hungary	DTC	25 Oct 1988	13 Aug 1993

Jurisdiction	Type of EoI arrangement	Date signed	Date entered into force/status
Iceland	TIEA	14 Dec 2011	14 Nov 2012
India	DTC	8 Sep 2011	21 June 2013
Korea	DTC	29 Nov 2011	22 Jan 2013
Liechtenstein	DTC	18 Oct 2010	3 Sep 2012
Malta	DTC	11 Mar 2011	13 Dec 2012
Mexico	DTC	14 Aug 2009	1 Jan 2011
Netherlands	TIEA	24 Oct 2012	
Norway	TIEA	14 Dec 2011	30 Jan 2014
Portugal	DTC	30 Nov 2009	13 Sep 2012
Romania	DTC	14 Sep 2012	22 Oct 2014
Spain	DTC	9 Oct 2009	24 Apr 2011
Sweden	TIEA	14 Dec 2011	Not in force. Ratified by Uruguay on 24 Aug 2012
Switzerland	DTC	18 Oct 2010	28 Dec 2011
Viet Nam	DTC	9 Dec 2013	
United Arab Emirates	DTC	10 Oct 2014	
United Kingdom	TIEA	14 Oct 2013	

Annex 3: List of all laws, regulations and other material received

Legislation pertaining to exchange of information on tax matters

Law 18 083 modified by Law 18 718 of 03.01.2011

Decree No. 313/011 amended by Decree No. 253/012 of 08.08.2012

Fiscal Legislation and Regulations

Tax Code

Organised Text of 1996 Title 4 (Business Activity Tax Law)

BCU Regulations on reporting obligations

BCU Circulars 1 878 (02.10.2003), 1 978 (27.11.2007), 1 993 (17.06.2008), 1 995 (14.07.2008)

Law 18 803 of 27/12/2006 (Tax Reform)

Law No. 18 930 of 17.07.2012 (bearer shares, foreign companies)

Law No 19 288 of 17.10.2014 (bearer shares)

Decree No 378/013 of 26 November 2013

Decree No. 247/012 of 02.08.2012

Decree No. 597/988 amended by Decree No. 242/012 of 01.08.2012

Decree 150/2007 modified by Decree law 208/2007 (Company Tax Law)

Decree 597/1988 (Information required on tax registration by the DGI)

DGI Resolution 1 859/2008 (FTZ Tax Return Requirements)

Primary government authorities

Uruguayan Constitution

Law 15 982 of 18.10.1988 (General Procedural Code)

Commercial laws

Law 16 060 of 01.11.1989 (Business Partnerships)

Decree 103 of 14.03.1991 (Accounting Statements of Business Partnerships)

Law 18 172 of 31.08.2007(Forbiddance of bearer shares in certain partnerships and business)

Decree 266/2007 (Corporation's Accounting Books)

Law 17 703 of 04.11.2003(Trusts)

Decree 516 of 2003 (Trusts)

Law 17 163 of 10.09.1999 (Foundations)

The financial sector

Law 16 327 of 19.11.1992 (Central Bank Law)

Decree Law 15 322 of 17.09.1982 (Financial Intermediation)

Law 16 749 modified by Law 18 627 of 16.12.2009 (Securities Market)

Law 16 774 of 7.10.1996 (Investment Funds) modified by Law 17 702 of 01.10.1999

Law 16 713 of 11.09.1995 (Social Security)

Law 17 835 of 29.09.2004 (AML)

Law 17 948 of 13.01.2006 (BCU Registry information)

Law 16 131 of 03.10.1990 (Investment Banks)

Other legislation

Law 16 871 of 10.10.1997(National Registry of Commerce, NRC)

Acordada 7 533(Public Notaries Regulation)

Criminal Code Article 302 (Professional Secrecy)

Public Notaries Regulations

Annex 4: Persons interviewed during on-site visit

Officials and representatives of:

- the Ministry of Finance,
- the Uruguayan tax Administration (Dirección General Impositiva (DGI)), including:
  - General Director and Deputy Director;
  - Tax Advisory Department;
  - Large Taxpayer Division;
  - International Audit Department;
  - Taxpayer Assistance and Guidance Division.
- the National Register of Commerce (NRC),
- the Central Bank of Uruguay (Banco Central del Uruguay [BCU]),
- the Notarial Council (Asociación des Escribanos de Uruguay),
- the National Internal Audit (Auditoría Interna de la Nación [AIN]), and
- the Association of Accountants.

ORGANISATION FOR ECONOMIC CO-OPERATION AND DEVELOPMENT

The OECD is a unique forum where governments work together to address the economic, social and environmental challenges of globalisation. The OECD is also at the forefront of efforts to understand and to help governments respond to new developments and concerns, such as corporate governance, the information economy and the challenges of an ageing population. The Organisation provides a setting where governments can compare policy experiences, seek answers to common problems, identify good practice and work to co-ordinate domestic and international policies.

The OECD member countries are: Australia, Austria, Belgium, Canada, Chile, the Czech Republic, Denmark, Estonia, Finland, France, Germany, Greece, Hungary, Iceland, Ireland, Israel, Italy, Japan, Korea, Luxembourg, Mexico, the Netherlands, New Zealand, Norway, Poland, Portugal, the Slovak Republic, Slovenia, Spain, Sweden, Switzerland, Turkey, the United Kingdom and the United States. The European Union takes part in the work of the OECD.

OECD Publishing disseminates widely the results of the Organisation's statistics gathering and research on economic, social and environmental issues, as well as the conventions, guidelines and standards agreed by its members.

OECD PUBLISHING, 2, rue André-Pascal, 75775 PARIS CEDEX 16
(23 2015 10 1 P) ISBN 978-92-64-23165-8 – 2015-01

www.ingramcontent.com/pod-product-compliance
Ingram Content Group UK Ltd.
Pitfield, Milton Keynes, MK11 3LW, UK
UKHW060017051026
15591UKWH00003B/252
* 9 7 8 9 2 6 4 2 3 1 6 5 8 *